Storytimes...
Plus!

Kay Lincycomb

Neal-Schuman Publishers, Inc.

New York

London

Published by Neal-Schuman Publishers, Inc.
100 William Street, Suite 2004
New York, NY 10038-4512

Printed and bound in the United States of America.

The paper used in this publication meets the minimum requirements of American National Standard for Information Sciences—Permanence of Paper for Printed Library Materials, ANSI Z39.48-1992.

ISBN-13: 978-1-55570-583-1
ISBN-10: 1-55570-583-9

Library of Congress Cataloging-in-Publication Data

Lincycomb, Kay.
  Storytimes—plus! / Kay Lincycomb.
      p.   cm.
  Includes bibliographical references and index.
  ISBN 1–55570–583–9 (alk. paper)
  1. Children's libraries—Activity programs—United States.   2. Storytelling—United States.   I. Title.
Z718.2.U6L55   2007
027.62'51—dc22   2006020636

For my parents,
Alton James Arnold and Mary Lyndelle Arnold

CONTENTS

PREFACE

Successful storytimes engage, entertain, and educate young readers. They play a crucial part in making the library—and the world of possibilities it represents—compelling. You want to offer creative, interesting, and enlightening programs that are easy to plan, simple to present, and flexible enough to fit to individual circumstances. I designed *Storytimes . . . Plus* to help you prepare and present a wide variety of programming concepts that make planning uncomplicated and presenting fun.

Every group of children is unique, a wonderful yet challenging reality, so the programs presented here are easy to adapt to please any audience at any time. In the public library setting, it can be risky to predict with exact certainty which type of group will attend. It's almost impossible to forecast the correct answers to key questions like

- Who is likely to show up?
- Will ideas prepared for one group fit another?
- How will each possible audience react to a particular book or storytelling technique?
- What happens if the entire family arrives and I need to engage children from the ages of two to twelve?

A winning storytime needs the ability to respond to the particular dynamics of each audience. You cannot rely on canned programming, because even the finest plans may need to change quickly. *Storytimes . . . Plus* programs are designed to meet this everyday need. The basic storytimes feature simple interchangeable parts and the "plus" elements are supplemental activities that can be added, removed, or modified on the spot.

The programs will appeal to a wide variety of readers and audiences, especially those between the ages of three and six. *Storytimes . . . Plus* should be useful to children's and school librarians in settings large and small, preschool and grade school teachers, and the parents of homeschooled children.

ORGANIZATION

Part I, "35 Complete Storytimes . . . Plus," offers 35 complete, ready to use, storytimes. Each is tied to a specific theme, from "Armadillo Antics" to "Vegetable Soup," "Boo-Boos" to "Peek-a-Boo," and "Dinosaur Stomp" to "Snail Trail."

The themes have been selected for their ability to both delight children and engage their creativity. A bit of repetition can be of great benefit to younger children, so I have tried to balance innovative ideas with familiar favorites.

Numbered themes begin with an overview of the entire list of activities from which you can construct a program. They all feature three essential components:

- "Rhymes and Songs" complement the program's unique theme. I wrote the words. Sing the songs to classic well-known tunes.
- "Storytime Picks" offers a list of annotated books that also works well with the specific theme. I have used all of these books in real-life settings and I promise they all appeal to toddlers, preschoolers, and elementary schoolchildren.
- "Crafty Corner" provides step-by-step instructions for constructing a simple take-home craft that also illuminates the theme and lets the children express some "hands-on"

Program 1

ARMADILLO ANTICS

This little creature, the armadillo, is fun to use with themes about rodeos, the West, friendships, or Texas. One of my favorites is to combine the armadillo with Christmas for a very different holiday storytime.

Storytimes . . .

1. Rhymes and Songs

Hungry Armadillo

Little Armadillo

Five Armadillos

I'm an Armadillo

2. Storytime Picks

Armadillo's Orange by Jim Arnosky

Armadillo Rodeo by Jan Brett

Armadillo Tattletale by Helen Ketteman

Armadilly Chili by Helen Ketteman

Don't Ever Cross That Road, an Armadillo Story by Conrad J. Storad

A Spur for Christmas by Florence Baurys

3. Crafty Corner

Paper Plate Armadillo

. . . Plus

4. Games

Tattletale Armadillo

5. Longer Projects

Painting Armadillos

Rodeo Unit

6. Tell Aloud

The Noisy Rock (See pages 145–147)

A Spur for Christmas

7. Food

Gummy Worms

Orange Slices

8. Tips

STORYTIMES . . .

Rhymes and Songs

Hungry Armadillo

Tune: Pop Goes the Weasel

All around the forest he goes,
Mr. Armadillo. *(Point around room)*
He sniffs around with his long, long nose.
(Point to nose)
Hungry armadillo! *(Rub tummy)*

All around the forest he goes, *(Repeat
motions)*
Mr. Armadillo.
He digs around with his long, long claws.
(Clawing motion)
Hungry armadillo!

All around the forest he goes,
Mr. Armadillo.
He flips around his long, long tail, *(Turn
and wiggle bottom)*
Hungry armadillo!

All around the forest he goes,
Mr. Armadillo.
He finds some food and he goes back home,
(Pat tummy)
Happy armadillo!

Little Armadillo

Tune: Little Bunny Foo Foo

Little Armadillo, running on the
prairie,
*(Move your hand in tune or use a stick
puppet)*

3

looked into the ranch house, and saw a
    pretty tree.
(Hand over eyes, look around)

Little Armadillo, running on the prairie,
    (Repeat)
called on all his brothers, *(Gesture to come)*
so they too could also see.

Little Armadillo, running on the prairie,
gave out all the orders, to his brothers three.
    (Point three times)
Little Armadillo, running on the prairie,
they gathered lots of pretty things, and they
    all agreed. *(Nod head)*

Little Armadillo, running on the prairie,
"Let's decorate this cactus, for all to come
    and see."
(Imitate putting up an ornament)
(Speak) And a cowboy came along, and
    said . . .
(Shake finger) "Little Armadillo, you need a
    star for that tree!"
Little Armadillo, running on the prairie,
They used the cowboy's shiny spur, to top
    their special tree. *(Point up)*
(Written to go with A Spur for Christmas)

Five Armadillos *(A Flannel Rhyme)*

Five armadillos digging in the ground.
One armadillo stopped and looked around.
    (Hands over eyes and look)

He saw a coyote and he started to run. *(Remove a flannel)*
He didn't think coyote looked like a lot of
    fun.
(Repeat, and count down through one)
Final verse:
Now no armadillos are digging in the
    ground.
Mr. Coyote stopped and looked all
    around.
He didn't see anything to fill his hungry
    tummy. *(Pat tummy)*
And he said, "Those armadillos sure looked
    yummy."

I'm an Armadillo

Tune: I'm a Little Teapot

I'm an armadillo with a hard, hard shell.
    (Knock on shoulder)
I have a pointed nose and I smell quite well.
    (Point to nose, and sniff)
I find the bugs with my long, long nose.
    (Wiggle hands like bugs)
And dig them out with my claws and toes.
    (Digging motions)

Storytime Picks

Armadillo's Orange by Jim Arnosky, 2003. Armadillo doesn't pay attention to any of his neighbors, until he discovers he needs them to find his way home. This story encourages friendships.

Armadillo Rodeo by Jan Brett, 1995. Bo, the armadillo, goes to a rodeo, and thinks Harmony Jean's new red boots are another armadillo.

Armadillo Tattletale by Helen Ketteman, 2000. Find out why the armadillo's ears are small and why it's not nice to eavesdrop.

Armadilly Chili by Helen Ketteman, 2004. No one wants to help Miss Billie Armadilly make her special chili. A Texas twist has been given to the classic story of the Little Red Hen.

Don't Ever Cross That Road, an Armadillo Story by Conrad J. Storad, 2003. A teacher armadillo instructs her students on armadillo history, facts, and safety.

A Spur for Christmas by Florence Baurys, 1999. When the armadillos see a pretty Christmas tree in a window, they want one of their very own, and so they decide to decorate a cactus.

Crafty Corner

Paper Plate Armadillo (Created by Pat Snell)
Materials: One 12-inch and 7-inch paper plate (not Styrofoam), black marker or crayon, wiggle eyes, glue.

Instructions:

Figure 1-1. Paper Plate Armadillo

1. Precut pattern pieces in advance for the younger children *(see patterns on page 167)*.
2. Fold the larger paper plate in half; cut two 1-inch slits along the folded center line for the feet.
3. Fold the small plate in half, and using the pattern pieces, cut out the legs, head, ears, and tail from that plate.
4. Cut the slit on the foot pattern, marked with the dotted line.
5. Insert the legs in the slits at the bottom of the larger folded paper plate, and staple or glue them.
6. Draw a mouth and nose on the head on each side and glue on wiggle eyes.
7. Cut the slit on the ear pattern, fold, and glue.
8. Insert the head on one end of the paper plate and the tail at the other end, then staple or glue the armadillo closed.

Alternatives: Paint the paper plates for a more realistic-looking armadillo. If you are doing the painting yourself, use spray paint in order to save time. If children help paint, make sure to use acrylic.

. . . PLUS

Games

Tattletale Armadillo
While sitting in a circle or row, whisper a secret message of your choice to the first child, then let that child repeat the message to one sitting next to him or her, and so on. Hear how the original message is changed when it reaches the last child.

Longer Projects

Older children will enjoy painting their own pieces for the armadillo craft (use acrylic paint) and making their own stick puppets to hold during the song *Little Armadillo*.

Prepare a learning center on Rodeos or the West. Add books about cowboys and rodeos. First grades and up can write a story and work on the craft or stick puppets.

Attend a rodeo, or have a mock rodeo where the children rope stuffed animals, ride stick horses, and so on.

Tell Aloud

The Noisy Rock by Pat Snell *(scripts on pages 145–147)* is a draw-and-tell story. Watch your drawing become an armadillo as you tell the story.

Make a flannel story from the book *A Spur for Christmas*. Hand out the decorations for the cactus, and let the children put them on the flannel cactus. An alternative would be to bring in a live potted cactus plant and let the children add materials to decorate it.

We wish you a Beary Christmas
We wish you a Beary Christmas
We wish you a Beary Christmas
And lots of good friends.

We wish you a Beary Christmas
We wish you a Beary Christmas
We wish you a Beary Christmas
'Til you're sleeping again.

Five Little Teddy Bears

Five little teddy bears filled with joy,
Hoping to be picked as a Christmas toy.
Santa picked the first one, and took him out
the door.
Now the teddies on the shelf numbered only
four.

Four little teddy bears filled with joy,
Hoping to be picked as a Christmas toy.
Santa picked the next one, to put under a
tree.

Now the teddies on the shelf numbered only
three.

Three little teddy bears filled with joy,
Hoping to be picked as a Christmas toy.
Santa picked the next one, for a child who
had the flu.
Now the teddies on the shelf numbered only
two.

Two little teddy bears filled with joy,
Hoping to be picked as a Christmas toy.
Santa picked the next one, and left in a
run.
Now the teddies on the shelf numbered only
one.

One little teddy bear filled with joy,
Hoping to be picked as a Christmas toy.
Santa picked the last one, and took him
away.
Now they'll all be with happy children, on
Christmas day.

Storytime Picks

Bear Snores On by Karma Wilson, 2002. Bear's friends try to wake him, so he can enjoy Christmas with them.

Bear Stays Up for Christmas by Karma Wilson, 2004. Bear's friends once again wake him up so he can enjoy Christmas. This time bear stays awake while his friends go to sleep and then awaken to a wonderful surprise.

Corduroy's Christmas by B. G. Hennessy, 1992. A lift-the-flap book based on the bear created by Don Freeman. Children will love guessing what is behind each flap as Corduroy gets ready for Christmas.

Is It Christmas? by John Prater, 2003. Little Bear learns about the many things that need to be done in order to get ready for Christmas.

Merry Christmas, Big Hungry Bear! by Don Wood, 2002. Little Mouse feels sorry for Big Hungry Bear and wants to make sure he has a present.

Snowbear's Christmas Countdown by Theresa Smyhem, 2004. Snowbear and his friends count down the 24 days before Christmas by listing their activities while getting ready for the holiday.

The Three Bears' Christmas by Kathy Duval, 2005. When the Three Bears arrive home after their Christmas Eve walk, they find that someone's gobbled their gingerbread, broken Baby Bear's chair, rumpled their bed, and left presents under their tree. And it's not Goldilocks.

Crafty Corner

Pom-Pom Teddy

Materials: Pom-poms of various sizes and colors (bear colors: brown, white, black, tan, etc), quick-dry glue or hot glue gun, wiggle eyes.

Instructions:

1. Glue two of the larger pom-poms together for body and add smaller pom-poms for ears, feet, hands, and nose.
2. Glue on two wiggle eyes.

Alternative: Use pipe cleaners or foam pieces for arms, ears, and so on. To use as an ornament, add string for hanging. For younger preschool children, you can use flat circles of craft foam and let them create a flat teddy bear on paper. This is easier for small fingers to manipulate.

Teddy Bear Ornament

Materials: Brown construction paper, wiggle eyes, stretchy string, materials to decorate.

Instructions:

1. Die cut a bear shape out of the construction paper.
2. Add wiggle eyes and decorate using glitter, shiny markers, popcorn, etc.
3. Tape or glue stretchy string at the back, for the ornament hanger.

Alternative: To save time buy prepackaged die cuts of bear shapes, or use your own pattern. Use different colored construction paper to make different kinds of bears (white for polar bear, black and white for panda bear, etc.). Use fun foam instead of construction paper for a stronger ornament, or laminate your paper.

Figure 2-1. Pom-Pom Teddy

Figure 2-2. Teddy Bear Ornament

... PLUS

Games

Bear's Asleep
Play this game like the traditional children's game "Statue." Children move around and pretend to be bears. Another child, who is "it," will call out the words "Bear's asleep!" at any point he or she chooses; then everyone will instantly stop all movement. The children must stay completely still until the first child calls out the words "Bear's awake." Anyone who moves before this will be out.

Longer Projects

Make a countdown Christmas calendar or use a regular calendar. Cross off each day in a special way, by giving a treat, telling a story, adding a teddy bear sticker, or whatever way or tradition you prefer.

Collect teddy bears and other small toys for underprivileged children. A classroom or homeschool family could adopt a family to buy gifts and food for Christmas.

Tell Aloud

Use the traditional action rhyme *Going on a Bear Hunt*. To fit more into a Christmas theme, use the adapted version *We're Going on a Christmas Tree Hunt (scripts on pages 147–148)*, or adapt your own version.

Food

Hand out teddy graham cookies, or make bear cookies by using a traditional gingerbread man cutout and adding two round pieces to the head before baking to be the bear's ears.

Tips

Combine the song *The Bear Slept On* with either book by Karma Wilson. It's fun to use flannels (or puppets) of the animals from the book as props.

Use five stuffed teddy bears as props with the counting rhyme *Five Little Teddy Bears*. Another option would be to make flannel teddy bears in different colors.

Program 3

BOO-BOOS

Everyone has an accident now and then. This storytime features a variety of small animals, toys, storybook characters, and Mr. Big Bad Wolf learning tips about safety and staying healthy.

Storytimes . . .

1. Rhymes and Songs

Did You Ever Have a Boo-Boo?

I'm Careful When

The Wolf

2. Storytime Picks

The Get Well Soon Book by Kes Gray

Healthy Wolf by David Bedford

Next! Please by Christopher Inns

Next Please by Ernst Jandl

Oh No, Ono! by Hans de Beer

Oops! by Colin McNaughton

Watch Out! by Jan Fearnley

3. Crafty Corner

Doctor's Kit

. . . Plus

4. Games

Wolf! Pig!

5. Longer Projects

Fairy Tale Comparison

Health Care Field Trip or Guest Speaker

Nutrition Chart

6. Tell Aloud

Puppet Play: *Once Upon an Accident, a Fairy Tale Filled with Peril* (see pages 148–155)

Fairy Tales and Folktales with Accidents

7. Food

Healthy Snack Basket

8. Tips

STORYTIMES . . .

Rhymes and Songs

Did You Ever Have a Boo-Boo?

Tune: Did You Ever See a Lassie?

Did you ever have a boo-boo,
A boo-boo, a boo-boo?
Did you ever have a boo-boo,
A boo-boo right here? *(Point to knee)*

A boo-boo on your knee,
On your knee, on your knee.
Did you ever have a boo-boo,
A boo-boo right here?
(Repeat with other body parts)

I'm Careful When

Tune: My Bonnie Lies Over the Ocean

I'm careful when I play with my skates.
I'm careful when I play with my bat.
I'm careful when I climb a tall tree.
I don't want a boo-boo on that. *(Point to head)*

I'm careful when I play with my skateboard.
I'm careful that I don't go splat.
I'm careful when I'm running bases,
I don't want a boo-boo on that. *(Point to elbow)*

I'm careful when I throw a baseball.
I'm careful when I play with my cat.
I'm careful when I run fast with my friends.
I don't want a boo-boo on that. *(Point to knee)*

The Wolf

Tune: London Bridge

The wolf, he saw the three little pigs,
Three little pigs, three little pigs
The wolf, he saw the three little pigs
In their houses.

The wolf, he went a huff and puff,
A huff and puff, a huff and puff
The wolf, he went a huff and puff
At their houses.

The wolf, he blew the straw house down,
The straw house down, the straw house
    down.
The wolf, he blew the straw house down.
Blew that house down.

The wolf, he blew the stick house down,
The stick house down, the stick house
    down,
The wolf, he blew the stick house down,
Blew that house down.

The wolf, he blew at the house of bricks,
House of bricks, house of bricks.
The wolf, he blew at the house of bricks,
But it held fast.

The wolf, he climbed onto the roof,
Onto the roof, onto the roof.
The wolf, he climbed onto the roof,
To get in that house.

The wolf slid down into the pot
into the pot, into the pot.
The wolf slid down into the pot
The pigs had placed there.

The wolf, he burned his furry tail.
Furry tail, furry tail.
The wolf, he burned his furry tail.
Pigs are safe now.

Storytime Picks

The Get Well Soon Book by Kes Gray, 2000. In this book with big color pictures, small animals get various boo-boo's but get better by following the doctor's orders.

Healthy Wolf by David Bedford, 2002. A wolf with poor health habits is taught to eat healthy and exercise.

Next! Please by Christopher Inns, 2001. Doctor Hopper and Nurse Rex Barker treat fellow stuffed animals in the animal hospital.

Next Please by Ernst Jandl, 2003. Toys wait in the waiting room to be fixed while they are counted down from five to one.

Oh No, Ono! by Hans de Beer, 2004. Ono, a small pig, is forever getting into accidents while trying to play with all his friends on the farm.

Oops! by Colin McNaughton, 1996. In this story told as a fractured fairy tale, a hungry wolf tries to catch clumsy Preston the Pig. But the wolf keeps getting into accidents along the way.

Watch Out! by Jan Fearnley, 2004. Wilf, a mouse, doesn't listen to his mother, which results in all sorts of accidents.

Crafty Corner

Doctor's Kit

Materials: Black and red craft foam, glue or staples, a sheet of letter-size paper.

Instructions:

1. For a pattern in making the main section of the doctor's kit, fold a sheet of letter-size paper (8½ × 11) in half. Cut two pieces of the black craft foam, placing the folded sheet on a folded sheet of craft foam with the folded parts together, so the two pieces are connected at the bottom, after cutting.

2. Glue or staple the sides together. The top will remain open.

3. Cut two handles from the black craft foam. Cut one cross shape from the red.

4. Glue or staple a handle to the inside of the doctor's kit, a handle on each side. Glue the red cross to the front of the kit.

5. Fill the bag with various doctor kit supplies such as Band-Aids, a tongue depressor, cotton swabs or balls, etc.

Alternatives: Use construction paper instead of foam.

Figure 3-1. Doctor's Kit

. . . PLUS

Games

Wolf! Pig!

Play this game like the water game Marco-Polo. Blindfold one child, who will call out "Wolf," and other children will then call out "Pig." The child who is "it" walks around until he or she catches someone and they change places. Use a limited area in which the children may move.

Longer Projects

For ages third grade and up, after performing the puppet play *Once Upon an Accident, a Fairy Tale Filled with Peril*, read traditional fairy tales and fractured fairy tales (or multicultural fairy tales) and discuss ways they are alike and different.

Study health and safety, take a field trip to a dentist or a doctor, or arrange a health care guest speaker.

With school-age children, talk about good nutrition and make a large or individual chart on the four food groups. Have the children keep track of what they eat at one meal each day and discuss how to improve their diet.

Tell Aloud

Once upon an Accident, a Fairy Tale Filled with Peril (script on pages 148–155) is a puppet play that can be performed with a minimum of two people, or the parts can be divided among many children. It can also be performed without puppets, with the children acting out the parts. It stresses health and safety characters based upon traditional fairy tale and nursery rhyme characters. Use the entire play or only the scenes you choose.

If you don't perform the play, then read nursery rhymes or folk tales that have characters in them that have had accidents or boo-boos, such as *Humpty Dumpty*, *Jack and Jill*, and *Itsy Bitsy Spider*.

Food

Serve healthy snacks from a basket such as Little Red Riding Hood would take to her grandmother. Let the children pack the basket, spread a blanket, and have a picnic outside or on the floor.

Tips

When singing the song *I'm Careful When*, hold up real props such as skates, a baseball bat, a stuffed cat, and so on. Another alternative would be to use flannels or pictures.

Combine the books *Healthy Wolf*, *Oh No, Ono*, and *Oops* with the puppet play *Once Upon an Accident* (or use just the scenes with the wolf in them), and follow with the song *The Wolf*, ending with the game Wolf! Pig! Before performing the puppet play, read any fairy tales or nursery rhymes that are used in the play which the children are not familiar with.

Read both books titled *Next Please*, have the children bring their favorite stuffed animal to show, and point out any repair that may have been done to their toy.

Program 4

BUTTON UP

Aren't buttons wonderful? When it's cold outside, you put on coats and jackets and button up tight; but when you're inside, buttons can be used for many different things.

Storytimes . . .

1. Rhymes and Songs

On a Chilly Winter Morning

My Friend Joseph Had a Coat

I'm Putting My Warm Coat On

2. Storytime Picks

The Button Box by Margarette S. Reid

Froggy Gets Dressed by Jonathan London

Grandma's Button Box by Linda Williams Aber

Joseph Had a Little Overcoat by Simms Taback

The Magical, Mystical, Marvelous Coat by Catherine Ann Cullen

Thomas' Snowsuit by Robert Munsch

Under My Hood I Have a Hat by Karla Kuskin

3. Crafty Corner

Button Picture Frame

. . . Plus

4. Games

Dress-Up Relay

Button Toss

5. Longer Projects

Button Math Center

Weather Chart

6. Tell Aloud

The Lost Button by Arnold Lobel

7. Food

Button Cookies

8. Tips

STORYTIMES . . .

Rhymes and Songs

On a Chilly Winter Morning

Tune: Mulberry Bush

We're getting ready to go out in the cold,
out in the cold, out in the cold. *(Shiver)*
We're getting ready to go out in the cold,
on a chilly winter morning.
Repeat with:
This is the way we put on our coat . . . *(Do motions)*
This is the way we put on our gloves . . .
This is the way we put on our wool hat . . .
This is the way we put on our scarf . . .
This is the way we put on our boots . . .
(Repeat first verse)

My Friend Joseph Had a Coat

Tune: Old MacDonald Had a Farm

My friend Joseph had a coat. E-I-E-I-O.
Soon that coat was torn and old. E-I-E-I-O.
With a snip, snip here, and a snip, snip there.
(Make cutting motions with fingers)
Here a snip, there a snip, everywhere a snip, snip.
My friend Joseph made a jacket. E-I-E-I-O.

My friend Joseph had a jacket. E-I-E-I-O.
Soon that jacket was torn and old. E-I-E-I-O.
With a snip, snip here, and a snip, snip there.
Here a snip, there a snip, everywhere a snip, snip.
My friend Joseph made a vest. E-I-E-I-O.

My friend Joseph had a vest. E-I-E-I-O.
Soon that vest was torn and old. E-I-E-I-O.

With a snip, snip here, and a snip, snip there.
Here a snip, there a snip, everywhere a snip, snip.
My friend Joseph made a scarf. E-I-E-I-O.

My friend Joseph had a scarf. E-I-E-I-O.
Soon that scarf was torn and old. E-I-E-I-O.
With a snip, snip here, and a snip, snip there.
Here a snip, there a snip, everywhere a snip, snip.
My friend Joseph made a handkerchief. E-I-E-I-O.

My friend Joseph had a handkerchief. E-I-E-I-O.
Soon that handkerchief was torn and old. E-I-E-I-O.
With a snip, snip here, and a snip, snip there.

Here a snip, there a snip, everywhere a snip, snip.
My friend Joseph made a button. E-I-E-I-O.

I'm Putting My Warm Coat On

Tune: Farmer in the Dell

I'm putting my warm coat on. *(Do motions)*
I'm putting my warm coat on.
Who, oh who, has a warm coat too?
(Point around the room)
I'm putting my warm coat on.

I'm putting my brown coat on. *(Do motions)*
I'm putting my brown coat on.
Who, oh who, has a brown coat too? *(Pointing)*
I'm putting my brown coat on.
(Repeat with whatever colors you wish to use)

Storytime Picks

The Button Box by Margarette S. Reid, 1990. A boy enjoys playing with and sorting his grandmother's button collection.

Froggy Gets Dressed by Jonathan London, 1992. Froggy gets dressed to go out in the snow and forgets to put on something very important, his underwear.

Grandma's Button Box by Linda Williams Aber, 2002. Kelly spills her grandma's buttons and everyone helps her pick up while sorting and counting the different types of buttons.

Joseph Had a Little Overcoat by Simms Taback, 1999. A Caldecott Medal book about how thrifty Joseph never wastes a thing. See how he recycles his old things as they wear out into something else useful.

The Magical, Mystical, Marvelous Coat by Catherine Ann Cullen, 2001. In her imagination, a young girl's coat has six magical buttons that do marvelous things.

Thomas' Snowsuit by Robert Munsch, 1985. This is about a little boy who doesn't want to wear his snowsuit. When his mother, teacher, and principal try to make him put it on, the results are surprising.

Under My Hood I Have a Hat by Karla Kuskin, 2004. A child shows what to put on when you go out into the cold.

Crafty Corner

Button Picture Frame

Materials: Precut cardboard picture frames with adhesive, buttons in a variety of sizes and colors, and a magnetic strip for the back.

Instructions:

1. Peel off the protective cover over adhesive and cover the frame with a variety of colors and sizes of buttons.

2. Attach a magnet piece to the back of the frame so it will stick on a refrigerator or metal area.

Alternatives: For a less expensive alternative, use cardboard frames without the adhesive backing, and use craft glue. Instead of using premade frames, die cut pieces of cardboard into a frame shape.

Figure 4-1. Button Picture Frame

. . . PLUS

Games

Dress-Up Relay

Use two sacks or boxes containing winter clothing (hats, coats, boots, etc.) and let the children race against each other to see who can put them on and off the quickest. An alternative would be to use shirts with lots of buttons and race to see who can button and unbutton the fastest.

Button Toss

Toss buttons into a basket and see who can get the most in. An alternative would be to toss rolled up socks into the baskets.

Longer Projects

For school-age children, create a math learning center using buttons. The children can then practice counting, sorting, adding, or subtracting with the buttons.

Keep a weather chart, and let the children take turns marking the weather for the day in some way such as adding a sticker or a symbol or whatever way you choose.

Tell Aloud

Tell or read the story **A Lost Button** from the book: **Frog and Toad Are Friends** by Arnold Lobel. Make flannel buttons (or use real ones) that match the story. Hand them out to the children so they can bring them up as you tell the story. Make a large flannel of Frog and Toad, and leave a place on Toad's jacket to try the buttons.

Food

Make button cookies by baking cookies and icing them to look like buttons. Spread on frosting, and then make the button holes with two or four drops of a different color frosting, candies, chocolate chips, raisins, or other edible decorations. Make cookies to match the cookies from the story **The Lost Button**.

Tips

Make flannel coats of various colors to use with the song **I'm Putting My Warm Coat On**. Another alternative is to have children stand up or raise their hands if they have a coat (or use a shirt or another item) the same color as that in the verse.

Combine the book **Joseph Had a Little Overcoat** with the

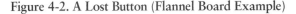

Figure 4-2. A Lost Button (Flannel Board Example)

song *My Friend Joseph Had a Coat*. Cut a coat shape out of paper *(patterns on page 169)* and cut it down to follow the words as you are singing.

Combine *The Button Box, Grandma's Button Box, The Magical, Mystical, Marvelous Coat*, and *The Lost Button*. Then sing *I'm Putting My Warm Coat On*, but change the words to "I'm *buttoning* my warm coat *up*."

The book *Daisy Gets Dressed*, by Clare Beaton, 2005 will be enjoyed by younger preschoolers. This will help them learn patterns such as stripes, wavy, spiral, checked, and zigzag. The book *Under My Hood I Have a Hat* is also good for younger children.

Program 5

COOKIE CRUNCH

What better sweet treat than a cookie? Decorate them, count them, and share them with your friends, but watch them carefully or they might run off.

Storytimes . . .

1. Rhymes and Songs

Five Little Cookies

There's a Cookie on My Plate

The Little Bitty Cookie

2. Storytime Picks

Cookie Count by Robert Sabuda

The Doorbell Rang by Pat Hutchins

If You Give a Mouse a Cookie by Laura Joffe Numeroff

No More Cookies! by Paeony Lewis

Twelve Plump Cookies by Larry Dane Brimner

Who Took the Cookies from the Cookie Jar? by Bonnie Lass

3. Crafty Corner

Gingerbread Man Ornament

Personalized Oven Mitt

. . . Plus

4. Games

Who Took the Cookie?

Hot Cookies

5. Longer Projects

Cookie Math Center

6. Tell Aloud

The Gingerbread Man

7. Food

Gingerbread Man Cookies

Magic Monkey Bananas

8. Tips

STORYTIMES . . .

Rhymes and Songs

Five Little Cookies (A Count-down Rhyme)

Five little cookies were sitting on a plate.
All the little children thought they looked just great.
One child picked a chocolate chip, and wished he could have more.
When that child was finished, there were only four.

Four little cookies were sitting on a plate.
All the little children thought they looked just great.
One child picked a pink one, and sat down beneath a tree.

When that child was finished, there were only three.

Three little cookies were sitting on a plate.
All the little children thought they looked just great.
One child picked a peanut butter, and he began to chew.
When that child was finished, there were only two.

Two little cookies were sitting on a plate.
All the little children thought they looked just great.
One child picked an oatmeal, because the raisins looked like fun.
When that child was finished, there was only one.

One little cookie was sitting on a plate.
All the little children thought it looked just great.
One child picked the last one, and when that child was done.
Mother looked at the plate and saw there were none.

No more little cookies sitting on the plate.
All the little children thought they had tasted great.
Now all the little children were sitting by the door.
And mother thought that she had better bake some more.

There's a Cookie on My Plate

Tune: There's a Hole in My Bucket

There's a cookie on my plate, on my plate, on my plate.
(Use hand flat like a plate, and point)
There's a cookie on my plate, a cookie right here.

I'm ready to eat it, to eat it, to eat it.
(Act as if eating)
I'm ready to eat it, to eat it right now.

That cookie's so yummy, *(rub tummy)* so yummy, so yummy.
That cookie's so yummy, it tasted so good.
Now the plate is so empty, so empty, so empty.
Now the plate is so empty. *(Hands out and open)*
Please Mom bake some more! *(Loudly)*

The Little Bitty Cookie (An Action Song)

Tune: Itsy Bitsy Spider

A little bitty cookie rolled across the floor. *(Rolling hands)*
I tried to catch it, but it rolled right out the door.
I was so hungry; I could not let it go. *(Rub tummy)*
I chased that little cookie, but I was so slow. *(Move arms as if running)*

That little bitty cookie rolled across the yard.
I tried to catch it, but it was so hard. *(Rolling hands)*
I finally caught the cookie, when it jumped into the lake. *(Jump)*
And that soggy little cookie, tasted oh so great. *(Rub tummy)*

Storytime Picks

Cookie Count by Robert Sabuda, 1997. A pop-up counting book, told in rhyme, with mice as the cookie chefs.

The Doorbell Rang by Pat Hutchins, 1989. Mom makes cookies for Sam and Victoria, but the doorbell keeps ringing and they must share the cookies with friends.

If You Give a Mouse a Cookie by Laura Joffe Numeroff, 1992. When you give a mouse a cookie, he'll want something else. Read about all the things the mouse wants.

No More Cookies! by Paeony Lewis, 2005. Florence and her stuffed monkey Arnold eat too many cookies and Mom says, "No cookies for a week." They come up with all kinds of plans to try to get Mom to change her mind.

Twelve Plump Cookies by Larry Dane Brimner, 2005. Egbert has twelve plump cookies and must divide them among his guests as they come to his door.

Who Took the Cookies from the Cookie Jar? by Bonnie Lass, 2000. Told in rhyme, this is a western version of the classic rhyme. A skunk hunts for his cookies among other animals and learns what they really eat.

Crafty Corner

Gingerbread Man Ornament

Materials: Brown construction paper, a gel pen and glitter pins, wiggle eyes, elastic string, and other materials for decoration such as markers, sequins, or glitter.

Instructions:

1. Use a die cut to make a gingerbread shape from brown construction paper or card stock paper.
2. Glue on wiggle eyes, and then outline the cookie in a white gel pen (to appear as icing).
3. Glue or tape a piece of looped elastic string to the back for the hanger.
4. Add a mouth and buttons with the glitter pin or a gel pen.

Alternatives: Instead of a gel pen, use a white crayon, marker, paint, or crayons; draw on clothing or just decorate the man. Use yarn or a pipe cleaner for the hanger, instead of string. If you don't want an ornament, put a magnet on the back to stick on the refrigerator or glue on a popsicle stick for a stick puppet.

Figure 5-1. Gingerbread Ornament

Personalized Oven Mitt

Materials: A solid oven mitt, pencil, sheet of paper, and fabric paint.

Instructions:

1. Let the children create their own design and practice on paper.
2. Draw the design or year lightly in pencil on the mitt. For younger children, do this for them, or just let them paint on the mitt, or help them outline their hand.
3. Using fabric paint, trace over the pencil design. Allow plenty of time to dry.
4. Add the year and child's name. (For younger children, write this for them.)

Figure 5-2. Personalized Oven Mitt

. . . PLUS

Games

Who Took the Cookie?

Sit the children in a circle with their hands behind them, and secretly give one child a cookie. Then repeat the rhyme ***Who Took the Cookie from the Cookie Jar,*** calling different children's names, until they find who has the cookie.

Hot Cookies

Take a toy cookie and play a hot potato game. Have children toss the cookie back and forth while music is being played. When the music stops, the child who has the cookie either wins or loses (your choice). Use several cookies at a time.

Longer Projects

In a school setting, to supplement lessons, create a learning center for mathematics. Make cookies from card stock, or foam, and have some cut into halves, thirds, and so forth. Let children draw a card telling how many people are coming to their house and another card telling how many cookies they have. They may trade a whole cookie for a divided one in order to divide the cookies evenly among their guests. Precede this with the books *The Doorbell Rang* and *Twelve Plump Cookies*.

Tell Aloud

Tell aloud, make a flannel, or put on a play of the traditional tale *The Gingerbread Man* or one of the many other versions. Die cut flannel shapes to match the characters, or make your own flannel board pieces.

Food

Make homemade cookies or gingerbread and decorate them, using a recipe or premixed dough, or use prepacked gingerbread cookies such as Little Debbie or some other brand. Make the Magic Monkey Bananas from the book *No More Cookies*.

Tips

Use flannel, toy, or real cookies to count down with the rhyme *Five Little Cookies*. Try to match the cookies to the descriptions in the rhyme.

Older children will enjoy reading the funny version of *The Gingerbread Man* from *The Stinky Cheese Man* by Jon Scieszka.

Bring a stuffed toy or puppet of the Cookie Monster and use it during the song *There's a Cookie on My Plate*. Have Cookie Monster eat a cookie.

Program 6

COOL COYOTE

Coyotes live in the West and are known for howling at the moon. In your storytime, will the coyote be nice or mischievous? The choice is yours.

Storytimes . . .

1. Rhymes and Songs

A Howling We Will Go

Five Little Coyotes

Coyote Pokey

2. Storytime Picks

Coyote by Gerald McDermott

Coyote Raid in Cactus Canyon by Jim Arnosky

Kissing Coyotes by Marcia Vaughan

The Purple Coyote by Cornette

Three Little Javelinas by Susan Lowell

Two Cool Coyotes by Jillian Lund

Way Out West Lives a Coyote Named Frank by Jillian Lund

3. Crafty Corner

Coyote Picture

Desert Sand

. . . Plus

4. Games

Coyote Hunting

5. Longer Projects

Colored Sand

Desert Diorama

6. Tell Aloud

Meet Tricky Coyote!

That Tricky Coyote!

The Rattlesnake, the Mouse, and the Coyote

7. Food

Banana Moon Pies

8. Tips

Isabel and the Hungry Coyote

STORYTIMES . . .

Rhymes and Songs

A Howling We Will Go

Tune: A Hunting We Will Go

A howling we will go. *(March in place)*
A howling we will go.
Heigh Ho, to the hill we go.
A howling we will go.

We're howling at the moon. *(Make howling noise)*
We're howling at the moon. *(Howl)*
Heigh Ho, to the hill we go.
We're howling at the moon. *(Howl)*

The moon is bright and round. *(Cup hands)*
The moon is bright and round.
Heigh Ho, to the hill we go.
The moon is bright and round.

When morning comes we'll leave. *(March in place)*
When morning comes we'll leave.
Heigh Ho, to our den we go.
When morning comes we'll leave.

Five Little Coyotes *(A Count-down Rhyme)*

Five little coyotes came out one night,
Because they wanted to howl at the moon.
One saw a hawk, and went for a walk,
He said, "I won't be coming back soon."

Four little coyotes came out one night,
Because they wanted to howl at the moon.
One saw a crow and decided he would go.
He said, "I won't be coming back soon."

Three little coyotes came out one night,
Because they wanted to howl at the moon.
One saw snake and began to shake.
He said, "I won't be coming back soon."

Two little coyotes came out one night,
Because they wanted to howl at the moon.
One saw a desert bat, but didn't stop to
    chat.
He said, "I won't be coming back soon."

One little coyote was left that night,
and he stayed to howl at the moon.
Everyone had gone home, and left him all
    alone,
and he said "I was the only one in tune."

Coyote Pokey

Tune: Hokey Pokey

Put your right paw in, put your right paw
    out,
Put your right paw in, and swish it all
    about.
Do the coyote pokey, and turn yourself
    around,
That's what it's all about. *(Clap, clap)*
Repeat with:
Put you left paw in . . . swish it . . .
Put your pointy ears in . . . flap them . . .
Put your sharp teeth in . . . snap them . . .
Put your fluffy tail in . . . and wiggle it . . .
Put your whole hairy body in . . . shake
    it . . .

Storytime Picks

Coyote by Gerald McDermott, 1994. This is a Native American folktale about a coyote who wanted to fly like the crows.

Coyote Raid in Cactus Canyon by Jim Arnosky, 2005. Four young coyotes cause mischief in the canyon.

Kissing Coyotes by Marcia Vaughan, 2002. Jack Rabbit brags he can do many things, such as kissing a coyote. When the other animals dare him to make good on his bragging, the results are very surprising.

The Purple Coyote by Cornette, 1999. Jim wants to find out the secret of why the coyote is purple.

Three Little Javelinas by Susan Lowell, 1992. This is a western version of The Three Little Pigs, in which these Javelinas battle a coyote instead of a wolf.

Two Cool Coyotes by Jillian Lund, 1999. Angelina, a friend of Frank the coyote, moves away, and now Frank must make a new friend.

Way Out West Lives a Coyote Named Frank by Jillian Lund, 1993. Frank the coyote and his friend Larry have adventures in the desert and see all sorts of desert creatures.

Crafty Corner

Coyote Picture

Materials: Dark blue or black construction paper, packages of stick-on stars, western-shaped die cuts, and crayons or markers.

Instructions:

1. Glue die-cut pictures to the construction paper.

2. Place the stick-on stars around a die-cut moon.

3. Use a crayon or marker to draw mountains, birds or crows in the sky, etc.

Alternatives: Cut mountains from construction paper. Make a frame to go around your desert picture. Draw and cut out your own coyote, or choose one from a book of patterns.

Desert Sand

Materials: Baby food or other small jars with lids, colored sand in several colors, die cuts, materials to decorate lids.

Instructions:

1. Spoon the colored sand in layers into the jars, packing it down tightly.
2. Tighten the lids securely and decorate the lids by using paint or markers or adding stickers.

Alternatives: For a desert scene, use a soda bottle, layered half way up, glue a coyote die cut to the side, and add a moon hanging by a pipe cleaner or yarn to the inside of the bottle. Prepare the lids in advance by using spray paint, or let the older children help by painting them with acrylic paint.

Figure 6-1. Coyote Picture

. . . PLUS

Games

Coyote Hunting

Seat the children in a circle, and start with one child saying, "I'm going coyote hunting and I'm going to bring (something like a rope, a horse, a water jug, etc.). The second child repeats the sentence and adds one more item, and this continues. This is good for memory practice. Give a prize or sticker to the child who can remember the most items.

Longer Projects

Let older children mix the food coloring and sand for the sand art craft. Be sure that everyone wears plastic gloves when handling the food coloring.

Making Colored Sand:

Materials: Swimming pool or other light-colored sand, food coloring, rubber gloves, and containers for mixing.

Instructions:

1. Put sand into a large containers (one for each color) and pour the food coloring onto the sand. The more food coloring that you add, the brighter the sand will be.
2. Using rubber gloves squish the sand and food coloring together with your hands until the food coloring is mixed evenly into the sand and it is the desired color.

Before it is dyed, let the children play with the sand. Pour some into a small inflatable pool. Outside is better, but I have put down large cut trash bags and let them dig through the sand inside, without having any sand get on the floor.

Use sand and a large box to create a desert scene diorama. The children can plan and bring material to put in the box such as plants, plastic desert creatures, and so on.

Figure 6-2. Desert Sand

Tell Aloud

Use puppets or make flannel board pieces to tell stories from the books *Meet Tricky Coyote* or *That Tricky Coyote,* both by Gretchen Will Mayo. These books include Native American folklore and give you several stories to choose from.

Make a flannel story using *The Rattlesnake, the Mouse, and the Coyote* found in the *Flannel Board Storytelling Book* by Judy Sierra, page 213.

Food

Serve banana moon pies so the children will have their own "coyote moon" to enjoy.

Tips

Make flannel die cuts of coyotes, and use them with the rhyme *Five Little Coyotes.*

Two good books, which because of the longer text will appeal more to older school-age children, are *Isabel and the Hungry Coyote* by Keith Polette, 2004, a bilingual retelling of Little Red Riding Hood; and *Coyote and Badger, Desert Hunters of the Southwest* by Bruce Hiscock, 2001, which teaches how badgers and coyotes hunt together.

Program 7

COWBOY CHRISTMAS

Children love to play cowboys. Instead of a traditional celebration, put on your cowboy hat and jeans, build your campfire, and have a good old-fashioned cowboy Christmas with all the trimmings.

Storytimes . . .

1. Rhymes and Songs

Prairie Christmas Tree

Over in the Prairie

Five Little Cowboys

2. Storytime Picks

Christmas in the Big Woods by Laura Ingalls Wilder

The Cowboy's Christmas by Joan Walsh Anglund

Cowboy Night Before Christmas by James Rice

Dream Snow by Eric Carle

Texas Night Before Christmas by James Rice

Twelve Lizards Leaping by Jan Romero-Stevens

3. Crafty Corner

Cowboy Mobile

Western Christmas Ornaments

. . . Plus

4. Games

Cowboy Games

5. Longer Projects

Introduce Little House Series

Dress Western Day

6. Tell Aloud

Going on a Trail Ride (See pages 155–156)

7. Food

S'mores

8. Tips

STORYTIMES . . .

Rhymes and Songs

Prairie Christmas Tree (*A Rhyme*)

The cowboys went looking for a Christmas tree.
On the Texas prairie, now what did they see? *(Look around)*
The first tree they found was much too small.
(Hand over hand indicating small)
The second tree they found was much too tall.
(One hand high, one low, showing tall)
The third tree they found was much too broad.
(Hand apart showing broad)
The fourth tree they found was thin as a rod.

(Hands close together showing thin)
The fifth tree they found looked just about right.
(Hands mid-distance, shake head yes)
So they chopped it down with all their might. *(Chopping motion)*
They took that tree home and set it up straight
and all the cowboys said it looked just great. *(Hands on waist, nod head)*
Then they took off their hats and circled around *(Do motions of taking off hat)*
the most perfect Christmas tree that they had ever found.

Over in the Prairie

Tune: Down by the Station

Over in the prairie *(Point away)*

27

Sitting by a campfire *(Hands warming on fire)*
All the busy cowboys *(Point around)*
were wishing they were home.

Christmas time is coming.
And they don't want to miss it.
(Shake head and finger "no")
Saddle horse, jump on, *(Slap hands once, jump)*
Now they're gone. *(Wave)*

(Repeat first verse)
Christmas time is coming,
and they don't want to miss it.
Round up all the cows now. *(Point around)*
No matter where they roam.

(Repeat first verse)
Christmas time is coming,
and they don't want to miss it.

Riding fast, and riding hard,
(Bop in place as if riding)
Now they're home. *(Spread hands)*

Five Little Cowboys

Tune: Five Little Ducks

Five little cowboys sitting on the range.
They all looked up and saw something strange.
(Look up and point)
Santa flew over and he stopped to say,
(Shake finger)
"Have a very merry Christmas Day."

The cowboys pointed way up high. *(Point)*
They had never seen a deer that could fly.
(Flap hands like flying)
Santa flew over and stopped to say,
"Have a very merry Christmas Day."

Storytime Picks

Christmas in the Big Woods by Laura Ingalls Wilder, 1997. This is a picture book, based on the Little House on the Prairie series but written in a picture book form. Laura describes all the things that go on at Christmas time, while living in the big woods.

The Cowboy's Christmas by Joan Walsh Anglund, 2004. In this book, originally published in 1972, the little cowboy and his imaginary bear friend get ready for Christmas. The text is in red and black ink, with the drawings in black depicting the little cowboy's real world and the drawings in red depicting his imaginary world.

Cowboy Night Before Christmas by James Rice, 1990. In this book, formally titled *Prairie Night Before Christmas*, Santa employs two cowpokes when his reindeer leave during a Texas sandstorm.

Dream Snow by Eric Carle, 2000. A farmer dreams of snow and he awakens to find it has actually snowed. There is a surprise ending when you find out who the farmer is.

Texas Night Before Christmas by James Rice, 1986. The classic tale "The Night Before Christmas" is retold in a Texas style. Santa arrives with a team of longhorns and fills children's cowboy boots.

Twelve Lizards Leaping: A New Twelve Days of Christmas by Jan Romero-Stevens, 1999. The song "The Twelve Days of Christmas" is presented in a western style, with western animals and items used for the gifts.

Crafty Corner

Cowboy Mobile

Materials: A variety of die-cut western shapes, a die-cut mobile hanger from extra thick cardboard, yarn, a pipe cleaner for the hanger, and glue or tape.

Instructions:

1. Precut pieces of yarn in two or three different lengths.
2. Thread the yarn through the holes in the mobile hanger, and secure to the top by tying or taping.

3. Attach the western shapes to the ends of the yarn with tape or glue.

4. Make a circle with the pipe cleaner, and thread it through the middle hole of the mobile hanger leaving a loop coming out of the top (for hanging), and bending the ends at the bottom to secure it.

Alternatives: Instead of a die-cut mobile hanger, use a piece of cardboard, and cut it in an X shape; or use a coat hanger and tie the yarn to the bottom, and wrap it in red or green pipe cleaners, ribbon, or crepe paper.

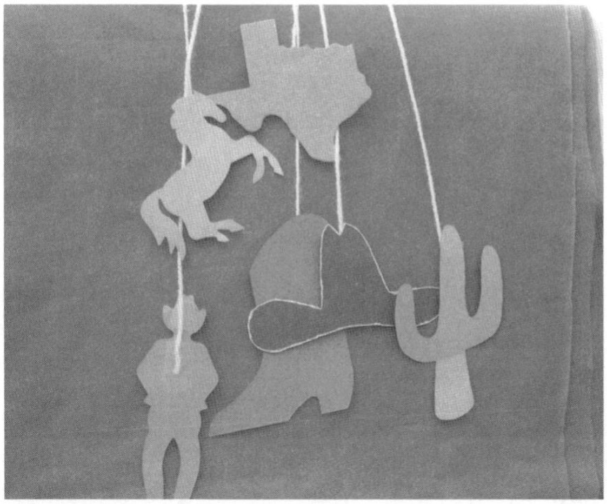

Western Christmas Ornaments

Materials: Western die cuts, materials for decoration (glitter, paint, sequins, etc.), pins for outlining (metallic, gel, glitter, opaque paint markers, etc.) and shiny elastic string in a bright color.

Instructions:

1. Glue or tape the ends of the string to the back of a die-cut shape, and leave a loop at the top for hanging on the tree.

2. Decorate the die shape with glitter, sequins, etc.

3. Outline with a pen of your choice (glitter, gel, metallic marker, etc.), and write the year.

Alternatives: Use yarn or a piece of pipe cleaner for the hanger. Cut your own western shapes.

. . . PLUS

Games

Cowboy Games

Play horseshoes and toss plastic horseshoe shapes to see if they can hit a mark. Use rope to try to lasso stuffed animals. Have races on stick horses.

Longer Projects

Read **Christmas in the Big Woods**, an unabridged chapter taken from *Little House on the Prairie*, to introduce the Little House series. Follow up by daily readings from the novels.

Have a Dress Western Day and come in cowboy clothing.

Tell Aloud

Tell the participation story **Going on a Trail Ride** *(see scripts pages 155–156)*, which is similar to **Going on a Bear Hunt**. The children make hand motions and noises along with you as you tell the story.

Figure 7-1. Cowboy Mobile

Figure 7-2. Western Christmas Ornament

Food

Make s'mores (melted marshmallows and chocolate between graham crackers), or use s'more-flavored Pop Tarts or s'more cookies, or just eat plain marshmallows.

Tips

Make a mock campfire with orange and red tissue paper arranged around a flashlight. Add real branches, or make them with cardboard rolls and markers. Sing songs, tell stories, and pretend to roast marshmallows, or eat s'mores while sitting in a circle around your campfire.

As an alternative to the hand motions in *Prairie Christmas Tree*, make flannel trees matching the descriptions in the verses.

Program 8

CROCODILE ROCK

With crocodile versus monkey, who will come out ahead? In your storytime, you can pit Mr. Crocodile against his ever-victorious opponent, Mr. Monkey, or choose to make the crocodile a more sympathetic fellow.

Storytimes . . .

1. Rhymes and Songs

One Little Crocodile

I'm a Little Crocodile

Baby Crocodile

It Snapped at Me

2. Storytime Picks

Copy Crocs by David Bedford

Counting Crocodiles by Judy Sierra

Crocodile Beat by Gail Jorgensen

Five Little Monkeys Sitting in a Tree by Eileen Christelow

What Time Is It, Mr. Crocodile? by Judy Sierra

Where's My Mommy? by Jo Brown

3. Crafty Corner

Crocodile and Monkey Door Hanger

. . . Plus

4. Games

Crocodile versus Monkey

5. Longer Projects

Papier Mâché

Crocodile Trip

6. Tell Aloud

Molly the Monkey and the Crocodile

The Monkey and the Crocodile

7. Food

Crocodile Krispies

8. Tips

STORYTIMES . . .

Rhymes and Songs

One Little Crocodile

One little crocodile out in the swamp,
Looking around to see what he could chomp.
(Slap hands together)
He snapped at a monkey, *(Slap again)*
But the monkey got away.
And the crocodile went home hungry that
   day.
(Hold tummy)

One little crocodile out in the swamp.
Looking around to see what he could
   chomp. *(Slap)*
He snapped at a frog, *(slap)* but the frog got
   away.

And the crocodile went home hungry that
   day.

One little crocodile out in the swamp.
Looking around to see what he could
   chomp. *(Slap)*
He snapped at a turtle, *(slap)* but the turtle
   got away.
And the crocodile went home hungry that
   day.

Last line:
One little crocodile out in the swamp.
Looking around to see what he could
   chomp. *(Slap)*
But all the little animals got away, and he
   didn't catch a thing.
So he had to get his dinner from the Burger
   King.
(Repeat with other animals if you wish)

I'm a Little Crocodile

Tune: I'm A Little Teapot

I'm a little crocodile, long and green.
(Hold Hands apart to indicate long)
I've the longest tail you have ever seen.
(Turn and wiggle)
If you go swimming in my swamp,
(Make swimming motion)
Look out for my teeth, *(Point to teeth)*
So you don't get a chomp! *(Clap hands)*

Baby Crocodile

Tune: I'm Bringing Home a Baby Bumblebee

Oh, I'm bringing home a baby crocodile,
(Hold hands as if holding a crocodile)
Won't that really make my mommy smile?

Oh, I'm bringing home a baby crocodile.
(Say) Ouch! It bit me! *(Shake hand)*

Oh, I'm throwing down a baby crocodile.
(Act like you are throwing it)
Won't that really make my mommy smile?
Oh, I'm throwing down a baby crocodile.
(Say) "Because it bite me!" *(Shake hand)*

It Snapped at Me

Tune: Three Blind Mice

See the crocodile. See the crocodile.
It snapped at me. It snapped at me.
I never ran so fast in my life,
As when that crocodile gave me a fright.
Did you ever such a scary sight,
As when it snapped at me, when it snapped
    at me?

Storytime Picks

Copy Crocs by David Bedford, 2004. Crocodile just wants to be alone, but all the other crocodiles continue to follow him in whatever he does or wherever he goes. When the crocodile finally gets away, he finds he misses his friends.

Counting Crocodiles by Judy Sierra, 1997. A smart monkey fools the crocodiles into letting him walk across the water on their backs by pretending to count them.

Crocodile Beat by Gail Jorgensen, 1989. In this story, told in rhyme, all the animals dance and sing by the river until they accidentally awaken a crocodile.

Five Little Monkeys Sitting in a Tree by Eileen Christelow, 1991. From the classic song of the same name; however, in this version there is a happy ending for the monkeys.

What Time Is It, Mr. Crocodile? by Judy Sierra, 2004. Mr. Crocodile plans his day, but later he changes his plans when he finds that he would rather play with the monkeys next door than eat them.

Where's My Mommy? by Jo Brown, 2002. A newly hatched crocodile makes friends while searching for his mother.

Crafty Corner

Crocodile and Monkey Door Hanger

Materials: A die-cut door hanger shape, various colors of craft foam, wiggle eyes, and a marker.

Instructions:

1. Cut the crocodile shape from green craft foam and his teeth from white craft foam *(patterns on page 170)*. For younger children, precut the patterns.
2. Cut the monkey shape *(patterns on page 170)* from two colors of craft foam (brown, red, orange, grey, etc.), making the ears and mouth one color and the rest of the face another color.
3. Glue the crocodile to one side of the door hanger piece, and glue the monkey to the other side. Add wiggle eyes to both.

4. Write the words "Come in" on a piece of white craft foam and glue it over the monkey. Write the word "Stop" on another piece of foam and glue it over the crocodile.

Alternatives: Buy precut door hanger shapes to save time, or cut a rectangle and add a string for hanging over the door handle. Use card stock or poster board instead of foam material. Use a die-precut monkey and crocodile instead of from the patterns. Change the words over the figures to "Please knock," "Enter," or whatever you choose.

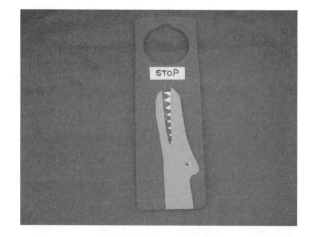

Figure 8-1. Door Hanger Side One

. . . PLUS

Games

Crocodile versus Monkey

Play this like a Red Rover game. Divide students into two groups. One side is the crocodile; the other is the monkey. Each group holds hands and forms a line, standing opposite each other. One group calls out in unison to the opposite team: "Crocodile, Crocodile (or Monkey, Monkey), let (someone's name) come over." The child who is called runs and tries to break through the line at the point where any two children are holding hands. If the children who are called over cannot break through, then they stay with that team; if they do break through, then they may take any child back to their own team. Play as long as you like, or until one side has all the others captured.

Longer Projects

School-age children can make a papier mâché crocodile or a piñata. For those who don't mind a mess, instructions can be found in craft books, or doing a subject search on the Internet will result in many choices.

Children will enjoy taking a field trip to a zoo, an aquarium, or a wildlife park to see a live crocodile.

Tell Aloud

From the book *Fold-and-Cut Stories and Fingerplays* by Marj Hart, use the story *Molly the Monkey and the Crocodile* on pages 18–24. A piece of green paper will turn into a crocodile as you tell the story.

Make a flannel story from *The Monkey and the Crocodile* out of the *Flannel Board Storytelling Book* by Judy Sierra on page 196.

Food

Make Crocodile Krispies by using the recipe for Rice Krispie treats but add a small amount of green food coloring and cut them long and thin instead of square. Add eyes by using two red hots and dots of white icing or white chocolate chips for teeth.

Figure 8-2. Door Hanger Side Two

Tips

Let the children hold up various stuffed animals used in the **One Little Crocodile** rhyme. Snap at the animals as they hold them up, and let them help the animals get away by yanking them away or putting them behind their backs. At the end of the rhyme, bring out a hidden Burger King sack for a surprise ending.

Use a small crocodile puppet while singing the song **Baby Crocodile** or **It Snapped at Me**, and let the puppet snap at you.

Program 9

DINOSAUR STOMP

Dinosaurs are always mysterious, intriguing, and exciting. Stomp and roar along with this bunch of colorful, playful creatures that will stretch your imagination as they prepare to go to sleep, dance, and play hide-and-seek.

Storytimes . . .

1. Rhymes and Songs

Five Little Dinosaurs

Stomp! Stomp! Roar! Roar!

The Dinosaur Stomp

2. Storytime Picks

Dinosaur Friends by Paul Stickland

Dinosnores by Kelly DiPucchio

Find-a-Saurus by Mark Sperring

Flapdoodle Dinosaurs (A Pop-Up) by David A. Carter

How Do Dinosaurs Say Goodnight? by Jane Yolen

Saturday Night at the Dinosaur Stomp by Carol Diggory Shields

Ten Terrible Dinosaurs by Paul Stickland

3. Crafty Corner

Dinosaur Bookmark

. . . Plus

4. Games

Dinosaur Dig

5. Longer Projects

Dinosaur Center

6. Tell Aloud

The Horn Players

7. Food

Jell-O Dinosaur Egg

8. Tips

STORYTIMES . . .

Songs and Rhymes

Five Little Dinosaurs *(A Rhyme)*

Five little dinosaurs in the forest one night,
Heard a noise that gave them an awful fright.
The dinosaurs heard a loud and mighty roar,
One ran away, and now there are four.

Four little dinosaurs in the forest one night,
Heard a noise that gave them an awful fright.
The dinosaurs heard a roar and then one did flee,
One ran away, and now there are three.

Three little dinosaurs in the forest one night,
Heard a noise that gave them an awful fright.

The dinosaurs heard a roar and away another flew.
One ran away, and now there are two.

Two little dinosaurs in the forest one night,
Heard a noise that gave them an awful fright.
The dinosaurs heard a roar and one more began to run.
One ran away, and now there is only one.

One little dinosaur in the forest one night,
Heard a noise that gave him an awful fright.
He jumped into his bed, trembling with all his might.
That roar was Papa saying "Turn out that light!"

Stomp! Stomp! Roar! Roar! *(A Rhyme)*

Stomp! Stomp! *(Stomp feet)*
Roar! Roar! *(Raise hands and roar)*

There's a dinosaur at my door!
I see a dinosaur big and green.
He's the biggest thing you've ever seen.

Stomp! Stomp! Roar! Roar! *(Repeat actions)*
There's a dinosaur at my door!
I see a dinosaur and he's yellow.
My, oh my, he is a scary fellow.

Stomp! Stomp! Roar! Roar!
There's a dinosaur at my door!
I see a dinosaur with wings of blue.
He doesn't scare me, does he scare you?

Stomp! Stomp! Roar! Roar!
There's a dinosaur at my door!
I see a dinosaur and he's red.
I sure hope that he's been fed.

Stomp! Stomp! Roar! Roar!
There's a dinosaur at my door!
I see a dinosaur that is tall and grey.
I think now I'll run away.

Stomp! Stomp! Roar! Roar!
There's a dinosaur at my door!
I see a purple dinosaur and he loves me.
I think I like this one, because it's Barney!

The Dinosaur Stomp

Tune: Hokey Pokey

Put your right claws in, put your right claws
    out,
Put your right claws in, and swish them all
    about.
Do the dinosaur stomp, and stomp yourself
    around. (Clap, clap)
That's what it's all about.
Additional verses:
Put your left claws in . . . and swish them.
Put your sharp teeth in . . . and snap them.
Put your long tail in . . . and shake it.
Put your wings in . . . and flap them.
Put your whole scary body in . . . and
    stomp it.

Storytime Picks

Dinosaur Friends by Paul Stickland, 2000. A small dinosaur runs from creatures, but the creatures all turn out to be his friends. A short text makes this a good choice for younger readers.

Dinosnores by Kelly DiPucchio, 2005. In verse, the dinosaurs cause quite an uproar when they go to sleep at night.

Find-a-Saurus by Mark Sperring, 2003. Marty thinks there must be dinosaurs still around, so he looks for them but without much luck. The dinosaurs are there, but are cleverly hiding.

Flapdoodle Dinosaurs (A Pop-Up) by David A. Carter, 2001. This colorful, pop-up book combines colors, counting, dinosaurs, and a guessing game.

How Do Dinosaurs Say Goodnight? by Jane Yolen, 2001. Ten tired little dinosaurs show how they go to bed.

Saturday Night at the Dinosaur Stomp by Carol Diggory Shields, 2002. Dinosaurs have a party, and dance and jump to a rhyming text.

Ten Terrible Dinosaurs by Paul Stickland, 1997. In a rhyming text, ten sleepy dinosaurs drift off to sleep, one by one.

Crafty Corner

Dinosaur Bookmark

Materials: Different colors of craft foam, wiggle eyes, and a marker.

Instructions:

1. Cut dinosaur shapes *(patterns on page 171)*.
2. Cut strips of the craft foam measuring about 1¼ to 1½ inches wide and 6 to 7 inches long.

3. Glue the dinosaur shapes to the top of the craft foam strips, and glue on the scales.

4. Glue on the wiggle eyes, and draw on a mouth.

Alternatives: Use card stock, construction paper, or precut paper dinosaur shapes instead of craft foam. Use popsicle sticks (painted) or ribbon instead of the foam strips for the marker.

Figure 9-1. Dinosaur Bookmarks

... PLUS

Games

Dinosaur Dig

Pick two children, and have each secretly choose a dinosaur. Then play a game similar to London Bridge by having those two children make an arch with their hands and the other children walk under the arch, while singing the following song:

The Dinosaur Dig Song

Tune: London Bridge

We're digging up a dinosaur, dinosaur, dinosaur.
We're digging up a dinosaur. Oh what will it be?

We'll take a shovel and dig it up, dig it up, dig it up.
We'll take a shovel and dig it up.
Oh, what will it be? *(Drop arms)*

When the song is over, the two children drop their arms and capture the child who is currently under their arms. The captured child is taken aside and given a choice between the two different dinosaurs, and stands behind the child whose dinosaur name they picked. Begin again, until all the children have been captured, and at that point, the children have a tug of war to see which team wins.

Longer Projects

Make a science learning center on dinosaurs and dinosaur bones. Include books and projects about dinosaurs. For older children, include a dinosaur model to put together or instructions on making an origami dinosaur. Provide markers and crayons for the younger ones to create their own dinosaur. Add books such as **Bones, Bones, Dinosaur Bones** by Byron Barton, 1990, or **Dinosaur Bones** by Bob Barner, 2001.

Tell Aloud

The draw-and-tell story **The Horn Players** becomes a triceratops. Find this story in *Frog's Riddles and Other Draw-and-Tell Stories* by Richard Thompson.

Food

Make Jell-O in an egg-shaped mold, and put a candy dinosaur inside before it firms completely. Serve shaped dinosaur candy or egg-shaped candy to represent dinosaur eggs. Homeschoolers will enjoy starting the day with oatmeal containing dinosaur eggs that dissolve into tiny dinosaurs.

Tips

Make flannel dinosaurs to use to count down with the rhyme *Five Little Dinosaurs*. Make a larger one for "Papa" (or use a puppet).

Use puppets, stuffed animals, finger puppets, or flannels, and match the dinosaurs in each verse of the rhyme *Stomp! Stomp! Roar! Roar!* Use a Barney doll or puppet for the purple dinosaur.

Program 10

EXTRAORDINARY EGGS

Whether it's hatching eggs, following the adventures of animated talking eggs, or munching breakfast, eggs make a yummy scrumptious storytime.

Storytimes . . .

1. Rhymes and Songs

It's Quacking Time

Twelve Little Eggs

Two Eggs Please!

Eggbert

The White Round Egg

2. Storytime Picks

Daisy and the Egg by Jane Simmons

Eggbert, the Slightly Cracked Egg by Tom Ross

Green Eggs and Ham by Dr. Seuss

Guji Guji by Chih-Yuan Chen

Hunwick's Egg by Mem Fox

It's Quacking Time by Martin Waddell

Two Eggs, Please by Sarah Weeks

3. Crafty Corner

Egg Man

. . . Plus

4. Games

Egg Race

5. Longer Projects

Egg Center

Farm Field Trip

6. Tell Aloud

Jack and the Beanstalk

The Ugly Duckling

7. Food

Egg-Shaped Candy

8. Tips

STORYTIMES . . .

Rhymes and Songs

It's Quacking Time (A Rhyme)

It's quacking time, it's quacking time,
When the duck egg goes crack, it's quacking
    time.
(Flap arms and quack)

It's clucking time, it's clucking time,
When the hen egg goes crack, it's clucking
    time.
(Repeat using different bird or animal sounds)

It's tweeting time, it's tweeting time,
When the robin egg goes crack, it tweeting
    time.

It's honking time, it's honking time,
When the goose egg goes crack, it's honking
    time.

It's gobbling time, it's gobbling time.
When the turkey egg goes crack, it's gobbling
    time.

It's snapping time, it's snapping time.
When the alligator egg goes crack, it's snap-
    ping time.

Twelve Little Eggs (A Counting Rhyme)

There are 12 little eggs in the carton
    today.
I'm going to fix myself a breakfast tray.
Crack! (Slap fist against open hand)
Splat! (Slap hands together)

Sizzle! (*Wiggle fingers, drawing out the sizzle sound*)
And flop! (*Reverse hands and slap together*)
White on the bottom and yellow on top.
(*Repeat and count down to one*)

Now there are no more eggs in the carton today.
I've eaten all the eggs on my breakfast tray.
Crack, splat, sizzle and flop (*Do motions*)
Now I'm so full, guess I better stop. (*Rub stomach*)

Two Eggs Please!

Tune: Three Blind Mice

Two eggs please! Two eggs please!
Sunny side up, Sunny side up,
Scrambled, or poached or deviled or fried.
Over easy, boiled hard or boiled soft inside.
With bacon or hash browns or toast as a side.
Two eggs please!

Eggbert

Tune: Bingo

There was an egg that had a crack.
And Eggbert was his name-oh!
E-g-g-b-e-r-t
E-g-g-b-e-r-t
E-g-g-b-e-r-t
and Eggbert was his name-oh!

There was an egg that had a crack.
And Eggbert was his name-oh!
(*Clap*) g-g-b-e-r-t
(*Clap*) g-g-b-e-r-t
(*Clap*) g-g-b-e-r-t
and Eggbert was his name-oh!
(*Repeat, each time taking away one letter and adding one clap*)

The White Round Egg

Tune: Three Blind Mice

The white round egg, the white round egg,
With one small crack, with one small crack,
He rolls out of the egg bin, and then out the door.
They told him he could not stay there anymore.
They drove him away so he left to explore.
The white round egg, the white round egg.

The white round egg, the white round egg,
With one small crack, with one small crack,
He went round the world and he saw many cracks.
He painted their beauty and then sent them the facts.
He found difference is good, so he can now relax,
The white round egg, the white round egg.

Storytime Picks

Daisy and the Egg by Jane Simmons, 2000. Daisy, the duck, is waiting for her little brother or sister to hatch, and will not leave the egg no matter what.

Eggbert, the Slightly Cracked Egg by Tom Ross, 1994. Eggbert is driven from the refrigerator because he has a crack in his shell. He travels around the world and finds that many beautiful things in the world are cracked, and he learns to be happy just the way he is.

Green Eggs and Ham by Dr. Seuss, 1960. The classic favorite story of Sam I Am who is trying to convince an unnamed creature to try a dish he thinks he dislikes but has never tasted.

Guji Guji by Chih-Yuan Chen, 2004. A mother goose hatches a crocodile egg and raises Guji Guji as one of her own ducklings.

Hunwick's Egg by Mem Fox, 2005. Hunwick, a bandicoot from Australia, finds an egg and tries to hatch it himself.

It's Quacking Time by Martin Waddell, 2005. Duckling learns that all ducks hatch from eggs as he and his family eagerly await his new sibling to hatch.

Two Eggs, Please by Sarah Weeks, 2003. Everyone in the diner wants two eggs, but everyone wants them cooked differently.

Crafty Corner

Egg Man

Materials: Various colors of craft foam, wiggle eyes, craft glue, and markers.

Instructions:

1. Cut an egg shape from white craft foam *(patterns on page 172)*, or use a die cut to make an egg shape. Cut the arm and feet pieces from any color you wish.

2. Glue on the wiggle eyes, feet, and hands.

3. With a marker draw on a mouth, and draw a crack on the egg, if you wish one.

Alternatives: To make an Eggbert, add the painter's hat and palette *(patterns on page 172)*. To make Humpty Dumpty, add pants, shoes, and a hat. Substitute construction paper or card stock for the foam, and color the eggs with paint, markers, or crayons.

Figure 10-1. Egg Man

. . . PLUS

Games

Egg Race

Place styrofoam balls (for eggs) on plastic spoons, and race to see who can make it to the finish line the quickest or who can make it the longest distance without dropping their egg. Try tossing the styrofoam balls back and forth to catch them.

Longer Projects

Create an egg learning center and study the hatching of eggs. Order hatching eggs and an incubator so the children can watch an egg hatch (do a subject search on the Internet or check with a nearby farm). Hen eggs take around 21 days to hatch. Show pictures of the inside of an egg as it develops, and put out books on eggs, farms, and related topics. This can supplement classroom lessons on farm life or embryo development.

Take a field trip to a farm that raises chickens so the children can see live chickens and the hens in their nests.

Tell Aloud

Tell the story, make a flannel, or put on a play of the classic fairy tales with eggs such as *Jack and the Beanstalk* (which includes the goose that lays the golden eggs) or *The Ugly Duckling*.

Food

Try some of many types of egg-shaped candy. Homeschoolers can experiment with cooking eggs in many different ways; don't forget egg salad and deviled eggs. There are also many egg-shaped candies to choose from, especially during Easter time.

Tips

Combine the books *It's Quacking Time*, *Guji Guji*, and *Daisy and the Egg* with the rhyme *It's Quacking Time*. Make a list of all the creatures you can think of that lay eggs.

If the children are not familiar with the famous cracks mentioned in *Eggbert*, spend additional time to talk about and show pictures of them.

Combine the song *Two Eggs Please!* with the book of the same name. Make a list of every way you can think of to fix eggs.

Older children (school age) will enjoy reading the book *Humpty Dumpty Egg-Splodes* by Kevin O'Malley, 2001. This is a funny fractured fairy tale about an enormous egg that goes on a rampage against the folks in fairy tale land.

Program 11

FOOD FUN

Food can be a lot of fun. You can choose stories about good or bad manners, foods you like or dislike, or even enormous or very strange appetites.

Storytimes . . .

1. Rhymes and Songs

I Never Will Eat

Alphabet Soup

Marvin Wanted More

2. Storytime Picks

Eat! Cried Little Pig by Jonathan London

Food for Thought by Joost Elffers

Froggy Eats Out by Jonathan London

How Do Dinosaurs Eat Their Food? by Jane Yolen

I Will Never NOT EVER Eat a Tomato by Lauren Child

Marvin Wanted More! by Joseph Theobald

Never Let Your Cat Make Lunch for You by Lee Harris

3. Crafty Corner

Napkin Rings

. . . Plus

4. Games

The Nose Knows

5. Longer Projects

Tea Party

Vegetable Creations

6. Tell Aloud

The Little Red Hen

The Castaways

7. Food

Unusual Food

8. Tips

STORYTIMES . . .

Rhymes and Songs

I Never Will Eat

Tune: My Bonnie Lies Over the Ocean

I never will eat a tomato. *(Shake finger)*
I never will eat a green bean.
I never will eat that potato.
So please take back these veggies from me.
(Push away with hands)

I never will eat cauliflower.
I never will eat broccoli.
I never will eat that cucumber.
So please take back these veggies from me.

I never will eat a zucchini.
I never will eat all those peas.
I never will eat that big radish.
So please take back these veggies
from me.

Alphabet Soup

Tune: Mulberry Bush

Oh I wish I had some alphabet soup,
alphabet soup, alphabet soup,
Oh I wish I had some alphabet soup,
So I can spell many things.

My bowl of soup has A-B-C, A-B-C, A-B-C.
My bowl of soup has A-B-C; D-E-F,
and now here's G.

I take my spoon and swirl it around,
swirl it around, swirl it around.
I wonder what things I could spell,
With H-I-J, and K and L.

I take my spoon and scoop it up,
scoop it up, scoop it up.
I take my spoon, what do I see,
Here's M-N-O, and now here's P.

I am eating all the words I make,
words I make, words I make.
Here's Q-R-S and T and U.
Now wouldn't you like to spell some too?

I'll spell for you and you'll spell for me,
spell for me, spell for me.
I'll spell for you and you'll spell for me,
here's V-W-X and Y and Z.

Marvin Wanted More

Tune: Itsy Bitsy Spider

Marvin was a sheep who was very, very small.
He ate and ate and ate so that he would
    grow so tall.
He ate up all the grass and he was so very
    pleased.
But all the other sheep cried "Marvin, slow
    down please!"
(Speaking) But Marvin wanted more.

Marvin was a sheep who was very, very
    small.
He ate and ate and ate so that he would
    grow so tall.
He ate up all the forest and ate up all the
    trees.
Until all the other sheep cried "Marvin, slow
    down please!"

(Speaking) But Marvin wanted more.

Marvin was a sheep who was very, very
    small.
He ate and ate and ate, so that he would
    grow so tall.
He ate up all the mountains and drank up
    all the streams.
But all the other sheep cried "Marvin, slow
    down please!
(Speaking) But Marvin wanted more.

Marvin was a sheep who was very, very
    small.
He ate and ate and ate, so that he would
    grow so tall.
He ate up all the world and he jumped onto
    the moon.
Now Marvin was alone and he was feeling
    very blue.
(Speaking) And then Marvin got sick. *(Make
    throwing up sounds)*

Now Marvin is a sheep who is very, very
    small.
But Marvin didn't care now that he was not
    so tall.
He had all his friends again, and too his best
    friend Molly.
And even thought he's small again, he feels
    so very jolly.
(Speaking) And now Marvin is happy!
(*Goes with the book* Marvin Wanted More!)

Storytime Picks

Eat! Cried Little Pig by Jonathan London, 2003. Little Pig's first word is "eat." He eats everything in sight while making a terrible mess, but since he is just a baby, he can learn better manners with Mom's help.

Food for Thought by Joost Elffers, 2005. The latest in a series of books in which different fruits and vegetable are cut and arranged to look like many different things. Enjoy all the books in the series.

Froggy Eats Out by Jonathan London, 2001. Froggy has trouble behaving and makes a mess when he goes to a fancy restaurant with his parents.

How Do Dinosaurs Eat Their Food? by Jane Yolen, 2005. Another "How Do Dinosaurs" book, and this time the dinosaurs behave badly in a restaurant and then demonstrate good manners.

I Will Never NOT EVER Eat a Tomato by Lauren Child, 2000. Charlie's little sister Lola is a picky eater, until Charlie finds a way to get her to try different things.

Marvin Wanted More! by Joseph Theobald, 2003. A small sheep eats to become bigger and gets carried away.

Never Let Your Cat Make Lunch for You by Lee Harris, 1999. Pebbles the cat cooks things for his owner that only a cat could love.

Crafty Corner

Napkin Rings

Materials: Cardboard rolls, paint, X-acto knife, materials for decoration.

Instructions:

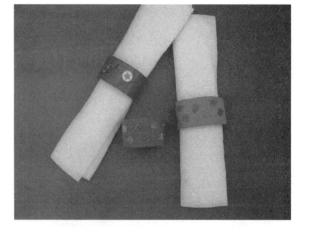

1. With an X-acto knife, precut the cardboard rolls into 1 inches to 1½ inches wide pieces.
2. Then have the children paint the rolls with acrylic paint or markers.
3. Decorate the rings to match any theme, holiday, or color scheme they wish by adding stickers, beads, glitter marks, etc.
4. Roll up pretty napkins and put inside your napkin rings.

Figure 11-1. Napkin Rings

Alternatives: Use craft foam or cardboard and glue or staple together. Give younger children prepainted cardboard to work with.

. . . PLUS

Games

The Nose Knows

Use scratch-and-sniff stickers or items hidden in a sack or container, and let the children smell the items without seeing them and attempt to identify them. See who can guess the most correctly. Try peppermint, red hots, vanilla, popcorn, and other aromatic items.

Longer Projects

Read the books *Froggy Eats Out* and *Eat! Cried Little Pig*. Have a discussion about manners. After making the napkin ring craft have a tea party and practice setting a table so they can help out Mom or Dad.

After looking at the creations in the books by Joost Elffers, duplicate some using real fruits and vegetables. Older children will enjoy making an original design.

Tell Aloud

Act out, tell, or make flannel board pieces of the original story of *The Little Red Hen*. Read other versions of the story.

Tell the story *The Castaways*, which is a draw-and-tell story about a hamburger and fries that is found on pages 58–63 of *Frog's Riddle* by Richard Thompson.

Food

Have an Unusual Food Day. Children can bring treats from home to share with the group. Bring candy or treats from another culture, something that the children have not tasted or heard of or something that looks unusual. Homeschoolers can cook meals from other cultures.

Tips

Use large flannel or cardboard letters with the song *Alphabet Soup,* and point to the letters as you sing the song or let the children hold the letter sign up.

The song *I Never Will Eat* was written to go with the book *I Will Never NOT EVER Eat a Tomato.* Make flannel vegetables *(patterns on pages 181–183)* and point to them as you sing.

Program 12

FRIEND FOR ME

Sometimes we don't realize how important our friends are to us. Whether you are playing with old friends or making new ones, this storytime helps show just how special and important friends are.

Storytimes . . .

1. Rhymes and Songs

Visiting Our Friends

Five Little Children

You're My Friend

2. Storytime Picks

Fox Makes Friends by Adam Relf

Rainbow Fish by Marcus Pfister

A Splendid Friend Indeed by Suzanne Bloom

That's What Friends Are For by Florence Parry Heide

That's What Friends Do by Kathryn Cave

Will You Be My Friend? by Nancy Tafuri

3. Crafty Corner

Picture Frame

. . . Plus

4. Games

Friendship Race

5. Longer Projects

Friendship Center

6. Tell Aloud

The Bremen Town Musicians

Flannel: Rainbow Fish

7. Food

Friendship Sandwich

8. Tips

STORYTIMES . . .

Rhymes and Songs

Visiting Our Friends

Tune: Paw-Paw Patch

We're going down the road to visit our
    friends,
Going down the road to visit our friends,
Going down the road to visit our friends.
We'll play all day, and then we'll come back.

We'll play with toys, and have a lot of fun.
Play with toys, and have a lot of fun.
Play with toys, and have a lot of fun.
We'll play all day, and then we'll come back.

We'll have a snack, and then play again.
Have a snack and then play again.
Have a snack and then play again.
We'll play all day, and then we'll come back.

The day is ending, and it's time to go home.
Day is ending, and it's time to go home.
Day is ending, and it's time to go home.
We'll play all day, and then we'll come back.

Five Little Children

Tune: Five Little Ducks

Five little children wanted to play.
They went to the park down the street one
    day.
One mama called, "It's time for a snack"
But only four little children came right back.

Four little children wanted to play.
They went to the park down the street one
    day.
One mama called, "It's time for a snack"
But only three little children came right
    back.

Three little children wanted to play.

They went to the park down the street one
      day.
One mama called, "It's time for a snack"
But only two little children came right back.

Two little children wanted to play.
They went to the park down the street one
      day.
One mama called, "It's time for a snack"
But only one little child came right back.

One little child wanted to play.
He went to the park down the street one
      day.
One mama called, "It's time for a snack"
But no little children came right back.

No little children in the park that day.
The children were at home, not out to play.
But soon the little children had finished with
      their snack.
Then all the little children ran right back.

You're My Friend

Tune: Frere Jacques

You're my friend. You're my friend.
We run and play. We run and play.
We are friends forever. We are friends for-
      ever,
Every day, every day.

You're my friend. You're my friend.
We run and play. We run and play.
We both help each other. We both help each
      other.
Every day, every day.

You're my friend. You're my friend.
We run and play. We run and play.
We love to play together. We love to play
      together.
Every day, every day.

Storytime Picks

Fox Makes Friends by Adam Relf, 2005. Little Fox is bored and tries to make friends with objects such as apples, sticks, and so on. When other young animals join in to help him, Little Fox soon discovers that they become his new friends.

Rainbow Fish by Marcus Pfister, 1992. Rainbow thinks he is better than the other fish and as a result is lonely, until he learns how to be a friend to others.

A Splendid Friend Indeed by Suzanne Bloom, 2005. Bear is annoyed with Goose, until he realizes how much Goose values their friendship.

That's What Friends Are For by Florence Parry Heide, 2003. Elephant's friends help him out when he hurts his leg and can't go visit his cousin.

That's What Friends Do by Kathryn Cave, 2004. Friends help each other, fight and make up, and show how friendship is a two-way street.

Will You Be My Friend? by Nancy Tafuri, 2000. Bird is too shy to be Rabbit's friend, until Rabbit helps him after they are caught in a rainstorm.

Crafty Corner

Picture Frame

Materials: Several large popsicle sticks, paint, glitter or glitter pens, beads and material for decoration, and glue.

Instructions:

1. In advance, paint the popsicle sticks in different colors.
2. Let the children glue the popsicle sticks together in different shapes. They can be made to hold one picture or several. Put out some examples to show the children, and encourage children to create their own designs.
3. Decorate the sticks with glitter pins, beads, stickers, sequins, or other decorations.

Alternatives: To save time, use precolored sticks. Have the children bring the picture or pictures they want to use and make the frames to fit.

Figure 12-1. Picture Frame

. . . PLUS

Games

Friendship Race

This is played like a three-legged race. Draw names or choose partners, have two children stand side by side, and tie their inside legs together with a cloth or something similar. They must coordinate their movements in order to run with three legs between them. Switch partners and race again. Vote on the team that works together the best.

Longer Projects

Friendship Center

For this center provide writing materials, paper, stickers, and markers or crayons so each child may write a compliment on a separate sheet of paper for every child in the class or group, and then decorate the page. Put each child's sheets of compliments together like a booklet and staple or tie the pages together with a ribbon. When the children receive their compliment booklet, have them decorate the cover of their own book.

Take pictures of the children so they can make a frame for them. Make a group picture of everyone.

Tell Aloud

Make a flannel story, or present a puppet show of ***The Bremen Town Musicians***. This is a story about how friends help each other out. Children can make animal masks and perform the characters.

Make a flannel from the book ***Rainbow Fish***. Make the Rainbow Fish large with shiny scales that stick on with Velcro so they can be pulled off and placed on the smaller fish at the end.

Food

Put out all types of sandwich fixings. Then let one child tell another how he or she would like the sandwich prepared, and then the listener will try to create that special sandwich. Do the same thing with ice cream sundaes or decorating cookies.

Figure 12-2. Rainbow Fish (Flannel Board Example)

Tips

Use die-cut flannel children to count down with while singing the song **Five Little Children**. If you have access to die cuts, have everyone create their own flannel child and decide on the color of hair, type of clothing, and other features that they want. They can then take turns using their own special flannel children with the song.

Skip or hop around during the first and last verses of the song *Visiting Our Friends*. Use toy and snack props during the other verses.

Younger children will enjoy the books *Biscuit Finds a Friend* by Alyssa Satin Capucilli and *Where Are Maisy's Friends? (A Pop-Up)* by Lucy Cousins.

Program 13

GUINEA PIG PARTY

What do guinea pigs do when you aren't looking? These furry little creatures have all sorts of adventures with their friends, both in and out of their cage.

Storytimes . . .

1. Rhymes and Songs

Five Little Guinea Pigs

The Guinea Pig

Guinea Pig, Guinea Pig

2. Storytime Picks

Brian and Bob by Jason Hook

Guinea Pigs Don't Read Books by Colleen Stanley Bare

John Willy and Freddy McGee by Holly Meade

One Guinea Pig Is Not Enough by Kate Duke

Sammy the Classroom Guinea Pig by Alix Berenzy

Twenty Is Too Many by Kate Duke

3. Crafty Corner

Guinea Pig (That can stand up)

. . . Plus

4. Games

Guinea Pig Relay Race

Guinea Pig Toss

5. Longer Projects

Make a Game

Guinea Pig Center

6. Tell Aloud

Fluffy the Classroom Guinea Pig

7. Food

Seeds and Nuts

8. Tips

STORYTIMES . . .

Rhymes and Songs

Five Little Guinea Pigs *(A Rhyme)*

Five little guinea pigs ran across the floor,
(Hold up five fingers, count down with each verse)
I scooped one up, and now there are four.
(Pretend to scoop one up, repeat with each verse)

Four little guinea pigs trying hard to flee,
I scooped one up, and now there are three.

Three little guinea pigs, one climbed into a shoe,
I scooped one up, and now there are two.

Two little guinea pigs, just trying to have some fun,
I scooped one up, and now there is just one.

One little guinea pig, see how fast he tried to run.
I scooped him up, now there are none.

No more little guinea pigs, trying to get away,
I scooped them all up, now they're safe inside their cage.

The Guinea Pig

Tune: Wheels on the Bus

The guinea pig eats his food
(Tap fingers and thumb in eating motion)
With a munch, munch, munch;
Munch, munch, munch. Munch, munch, munch.
The guinea pig eats his food
With a munch, munch, munch,
In his little cage.

The guinea pig likes to run *(Fingers as running)*

back and forth, back and forth, back and
forth.
The guinea pig likes to run back and forth,
In his little cage.

The guinea pig wiggles his nose just like that,
(Tap nose and wiggle it with your finger)
Just like that, just like that.
The guinea pig wiggles his nose just like that.
In his little cage.

The guinea pig likes to sleep all day long.
(Head on hands)
All day long, all day long.
The guinea pig likes to sleep all day long.
In his little cage.

Guinea Pig, Guinea Pig

Tune: Jingle Bells

Guinea pig, guinea pig, I just like the way

You twitch your whiskers and wiggle your
nose
When you set out to play. *(Wiggle fingers by
nose)*
Oh!
Chorus:
Guinea pig, guinea pig, I just like the
way,
You curl into a fluffy ball *(Hands cupped)*
At the end of your busy day.

Guinea pig, guinea pig, I just like the way
You run inside your great big wheel
When you set out to play. *(Twirl hands)*
Oh!
Guinea pig, guinea pig, I just like the way
You curl into a fluffy ball
At the end of your busy day.

Storytime Picks

Brian and Bob by Jason Hook, 2003. Brian and Bob are best friends in the pet shop until
they are bought by two different people. Find out how they end up together once again.

Guinea Pigs Don't Read Books by Colleen Stanley Bare, 1993. Although this is a nonfiction
book, it reads like a picture book and has adorable pictures showing what guinea pigs can and
cannot do.

John Willy and Freddy McGee by Holly Meade, 1998. Two bored guinea pigs escape their
cage, go on a great adventure through the house, and are followed by a house cat.

One Guinea Pig Is Not Enough by Kate Duke, 1998. Count the guinea pigs and watch them
in all their many activities on the beach.

Sammy the Classroom Guinea Pig by Alix Berenzy, 2005. When the children come in after
a weekend, Sammy makes an unusual sound and the children worry that something is wrong
with him.

Twenty Is Too Many by Kate Duke, 2000. The guinea pigs (from Duke's book listed above)
are back and this time they are counting down in their numbers.

Crafty Corner

Guinea Pig (That Can Stand Up)

Materials: Craft foam, wiggle eyes, small pom-poms, and cardboard toilet tissue roll or a
paper towel roll cut in half.

Instructions:

1. Cut the guinea pig body and ears from two different colors of craft foam *(patterns on
   page 173)*.
2. Glue on the ear, a wiggle eye, and a pom-pom for the nose.
3. Glue the cardboard roll to the back side along the bottom so guinea pig will stand up
   by leaning against the cardboard roll.

Alternatives: Use card stock instead of craft foam. Paint the cardboard roll. Make two guinea pigs and glue one on each side of the cardboard roll for a 3-D look.

Figure 13-1. Standing Guinea Pig

. . . PLUS

Games

Guinea Pig Relay Race

Take long strings of yarn and wind them around the room, putting the yarn loosely around chairs, desks, and other objects. Use at least two pieces of yarn so at least two children can race each other. Make sure both ends begin at the same place and end at the same place (tie them to something to keep both ends in place), but making each one go a different path around the room.

To begin the race, children put the yarn through the cardboard roll on the guinea pig they made for the craft and tie the end of the yarn on something to keep it in place. Someone says "Go" and the children then quickly pull the guinea pig over the yarn, through the room, following the yarn all the way to the end. The first one to the end of their yarn wins the race.

Guinea Pig Toss

Make or buy brown beanbags and glue on wiggle eyes and add felt whiskers so you will have a guinea pig beanbag. Take a large piece of green poster board or art board, and cut several holes around the edges for a pool table from the book *John Willy and Freddy McGee*. Stand back and toss guinea pigs into the pool table holes.

Longer Projects

Have the children create a more elaborate cardboard pool table for the game above with markers, felt, contact paper, and other materials. They can also decorate their own beanbags by drawing on the whiskers and other features and adding the wiggle eyes themselves.

Create a guinea pig center by adopting or borrowing a live guinea pig. Read the books *Guinea Pigs Don't Read Books* and *Sammy the Classroom Guinea Pig*. Then assign different duties to students daily for taking care of their pet (feeding, changing water, changing bedding, or exercise time, etc.). Make a chart to assign jobs each day.

Tell Aloud

Kate McMullan has a series of books entitled *Fluffy the Classroom Guinea Pig*. This series will make a cute flannel board story if you make flannel figures to represent the characters. An alternative would be to make stick puppets to represent the characters. Let the children act out one of the books with the stick puppets. There are Fluffy books for almost every holiday and classroom event.

Food

Guinea pigs like sunflower seeds and small nuts. Make snack bags with a mixture of sunflower seeds and nuts to hand out for a guinea pig snack.

Tips

Use flannel guinea pigs to count down while saying the rhyme *Five Little Guinea Pigs*. Make a flannel cage to put the guinea pigs in when you pick them up. For an alternative, use Beanie Baby guinea pigs or stuffed animals instead of flannel ones and put them in a box for the cage.

Read the book *John Willy and Freddy McGee*, follow with making the craft, and then play the Guinea Pig relay race game.

Program 15

HERMIT CRAB'S HOUSE

Do you love the ocean and collecting shells? There just might be a surprise in the next shell you pick up. Follow little hermit crabs as they go about searching for the perfect shell to become their house.

Storytimes . . .

1. Rhymes and Songs

Five Little Hermit Crabs

I See Hermit Crab

Snapping

2. Storytime Picks

Hector the Hermit Crab by Katie Boyce

A House for Hermit Crab by Eric Carle

Is This a House for Hermit Crab? by Megan McDonald

Moving Day by Robert Kalan

Old Shell, New Shell: A Coral Reef Tale by Helen Ward

Platypus by Chris Riddell

3. Crafty Corner

Hermit Crab Picture

Ocean Bottle

. . . Plus

4. Games

Put the Sea Creature on the Shell

5. Longer Projects

Fishing Center

6. Tell Aloud

A House for Hermit Crab

7. Food

Sea Creature Gelatin

8. Tips

STORYTIMES . . .

Rhymes and Songs

Five Little Hermit Crabs (*A Counting Rhyme*)

Five little hermit crabs ran across the ocean floor.
One crawled in a big shell, and now there are only four.

Four little hermit crabs looked to see what they could see.
One crawled in a small shell, and now there are only three.

Three little hermit crabs floated in the ocean blue.
One crawled into a wide shell, now there are only two.

Two little hermit crabs were having lots of fun.
One crawled into a long shell, now there's only one.

One little hermit crab looked around and saw
A perfect little shell so he grabbed it with his claw.
Now there are no more little hermit crabs on the ocean floor.
They all have a house now, and are safe behind their door.

I See a Hermit Crab

Tune: Pop, Goes the Weasel

I walked across the ocean floor,
the sand's between my toes.
Hey, I see a hermit crab, Oops!

There it goes.

I try to catch that hermit crab
to put him in my pail.
I do not think he wants to go, Oops!
He's in his shell.

I think I'll let that hermit go,
I hear his claws a-snapping.
I do not want a pinch from him, Oops!
Now he's napping.

Snapping

Tune: Frere Jacques

I see hermit crab, I see hermit crab

at my feet, at my feet *(Point)*
Snapping, snapping, snapping,
snapping, snapping, snapping,
At the beach, at the beach.

I see hermit crab, I see hermit crab
by my toe, by my toe.
Snapping, snapping, snapping,
Snapping, snapping, snapping.
There he goes, there he goes.

I see hermit crab, I see hermit crab
In his shell, in his shell.
He's found himself a home now.
He's found himself a home now.
He'll do well, he'll do well.

Storytime Picks

Hector the Hermit Crab by Katie Boyce, 2003. Hector the shy hermit crab makes friends when he finds a flower growing on his house.

A House for Hermit Crab by Eric Carle, 1991. Hermit Crab finds a new shell and decorates it with other sea creatures that he meets.

Is This a House for Hermit Crab? by Megan McDonald, 1993. A hermit crab tries many things to use as a home, but none seem just right.

Moving Day by Robert Kalan, 1996. In this story, told in rhyme, a hermit crab looks at many shells in order to find the perfect one to use for his home.

Old Shell, New Shell: A Coral Reef Tale by Helen Ward, 2002. Two hermit crabs each find the perfect shell just right for them.

Platypus by Chris Riddell, 2002. An adorable platypus tries to find the perfect shell for his collection but gets a big surprise when he finds the shell has a crab inside.

Crafty Corner

Hermit Crab Picture

Materials: Blue construction or scrap booking paper, construction paper or card stock in the shape of a seashell, a hermit crab shape *(patterns on page 175)*, brown sand, wiggle eyes, a marker, an X-acto knife, and a popsicle stick.

Instructions:

1. With an X-acto knife, in advance, cut a slit in middle of the blue paper. It should be big enough for the popsicle stick to slide through easily.

2. Children cut out the hermit crab and shell shapes. (Precut these for younger children.)

3. Spread glue over the shell shape, cover it in sand, allow it to dry as long as possible, and then shake off the excess sand.

4. Add wiggle eyes to the hermit crab shape, and draw a mouth on it with the marker.

5. Glue the crab to one end of the popsicle stick and slide the other end through the hole in the paper.

6. Glue the edges only of the shell shape, leaving the top unglued. Place the shell over the hermit crab. The crab should be able to move in and out of the shell when you slide the popsicle stick back and forth.

Alternatives: Use craft foam for the shell and crab. Use plain card stock and color your crab. Make small sea creature shapes and glue them to the shell.

Ocean Bottle

Materials: Empty plastic bottles (about the size of a .5 liter or smaller), green or blue food coloring, cooking oil, larger funnels, and water.

Instructions:

1. First fill the bottle halfway or a little more with water. You must pour the water in first before the oil, or it won't work.
2. Drop in a few drops of food coloring, put the lid back on, and gently shake the bottle until the color is evenly blended into the water.
3. Reopen the bottle and, using a funnel, fill it to the top with the cooking oil. Hint: pouring by placing the bottle in a large plastic tub or bowl will help prevent mess.
4. Screw the lid on very tight. Now turn the bottle sideways and rock it gently back and forth, and you will see the appearance of ocean waves.

Alternatives: Add small seashells, sequins, or small rocks to the mixture.

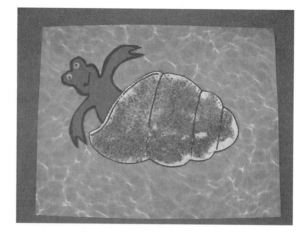

Figure 15-1. Hermit Crab Picture

Figure 15-2. Ocean Bottle

. . . PLUS

Games

Put the Sea Creature on the Shell

Play a game similar to Pin the Tail on the Donkey by drawing a very large shell on from poster board or flannel and attaching it to the wall. Make sea creatures (or use a pattern book) similar to the ones in **A House for Hermit Crab**, and put Velcro or double-sided tape on the back. Have each child, blindfolded, try to place a sea creature on the shell. See how the shell is decorated when all the children have placed their creatures on it.

Longer Projects

Create a fishing center for a fun way to assign duties, activities, or even give treats. Make a fishing pole by tying one end of a string to a stick and a magnet to the other. Then die cut shell or sea or creature shapes from card stock, stick a thin piece of magnet strip to one side, and place them, magnet side up, in a small wading pool. Catch the sea creature by lowering the magnet on the string until you can touch the two magnets together and the magnets stick together. Write or tape different things on the bottoms of the sea creatures such as prizes, treats, chores, or center or activity assignments so what the children catch will be a surprise.

Tell Aloud

Create a flannel story from the book *A House for Hermit Crab*. Make a large shell and hermit crab. Then make multiple flannel copies of the different sea creatures, enough for everyone to have one so they can put them on the hermit crab's house as you tell the story. If you choose to make a large shell, you can also use it for the game.

Food

Make green or blue gelatin in clear plastic cups to resemble water, and add any type of candy that resembles sea creatures, or just place a rounded spoon of whipped cream or whipped topping on top for a seashell.

Tips

When saying the rhyme *Five Little Hermit Crabs*, make flannel crabs and flannel shells that match the shells in the rhyme. Cover the crabs with the shells when the rhyme indicates.

Bring a shell collection to display. Let the children pick up and touch different shapes and kinds of shells. Small, inexpensive shell kits are easily available to order if you have no access to shells.

Bring in a real hermit crab so the children can observe what one looks like and how it behaves.

Program 16

KANGAROO HOP

How do kangaroos learn to hop, and why do they have a pouch? Tell stories about these amazing marsupials and everyone will have a hopping good time.

Storytimes . . .

1. Rhymes and Songs

Kangaroo, Kangaroo

Here We Go Jumping

Five Baby Kangaroos

Baby Kangaroo

2. Storytime Picks

Boing by Nick Bruel

I Love You, Blue Kangaroo by Emma Chichester Clark

Jump, Kangaroo, Jump! by Stuart J. Murphy

McGillycuddy Could! by Pamela Duncan Edwards

Polly Hopper's Pouch by Louise Bonnett-Rampersaud

What Did You Put in Your Pocket? by Beatrice Schenk de Regniers

When Kangaroo Goes to School by Sonia Levitin

3. Crafty Corner

Jumping Kangaroo

. . . Plus

4. Games

Kangaroo Relays

5. Longer Projects

Kangaroo Math Center

6. Tell Aloud

I Love You, Blue Kangaroo

7. Food

Pouch Sandwiches

8. Tips

STORYTIMES . . .

Rhymes and Songs

Kangaroo, Kangaroo (A Rhyme)

(Act out the actions)

Kangaroo, kangaroo, bounce up and down.
Kangaroo, kangaroo, touch the ground.
Kangaroo, kangaroo, make your ears go
    flop.
Kangaroo, kangaroo, now let's hop.
Kangaroo, kangaroo, bend down low.
Kangaroo, kangaroo, now jump just so.
Kangaroo, kangaroo, here are your great big
    toes.
Kangaroo, kangaroo, now here we go.
(Jump around in a circle)

Here We Go Jumping

Tune: Looby Loo

Here we go jumping high,
Here we go jumping low.
Here we go jumping around
That's how the kangaroo goes.

Here we go jumping fast.
Here we go jumping slow.
Here we go jumping everywhere.
That's how the kangaroo goes.
(Match jumping to verses)

Five Baby Kangaroos (An Action Rhyme)

Five baby kangaroos standing in a row.
    (Hold up five fingers)
And when they saw their mothers,

they jump just so. *(Jump up and down)*
They jump to the left. *(Jump left)*
They jump to the right. *(Jump right)*
One jumps in his mother's pouch, *(Big jump)*
to sleep throughout the night. *(Hands on cheek)*
(Repeat verses counting down 4, 3, 2, 1)

Now there're no baby kangaroos
Standing in a row.
They are all sleeping now; it's time for us to go.
They jumped to the left. *(Jump left)*
They jumped to the right. *(Jump right)*
They jumped down the road, *(Jump in place)*
until they were out of sight. *(Wave)*

Baby Kangaroo

Tune: Frere Jacques

I am a baby kangaroo.
I am a baby kangaroo,

Hopping is fun, hopping is fun. *(Hop in place)*
Hopping, hopping, hopping *(Hop around in a circle)*
Hopping, hopping, hopping.
Up and down, up and down. *(Hop matching verse)*

I am a baby kangaroo.
I am a baby kangaroo,
Hopping is fun, hopping is fun. *(Repeat actions)*
Won't you please hop with me? *(Point around)*
Won't you please hop with me?
We'll have fun. We'll have fun.

I am a baby kangaroo.
I am a baby kangaroo.
Hopping is fun, hopping is fun.
I'll hop on home to mama. *(Wave and hop)*
I'll hop on home to mama,
when day is done, when day is done.

Storytime Picks

Boing by Nick Bruel, 2004. A young kangaroo's animal friends, who also hop, try to teach him how to do it right. There is a pop-up surprise at the end, when the kangaroo is finally successful in jumping.

I Love You, Blue Kangaroo by Emma Chichester Clark, 1999. Blue Kangaroo is jealous of Lily's new stuffed toys, and worries that he isn't her favorite anymore.

Jump, Kangaroo, Jump! by Stuart J. Murphy, 1999. It's field day at animal school and the animals divide in different teams to participate in the events. Kangaroo is not good at the games until the jumping contest.

McGillycuddy Could! by Pamela Duncan Edwards, 2005. McGillycuddy, the kangaroo, doesn't seem to be able to do things the other farm animals do. But when a fox attacks the other animals, they find that McGillycuddy is the only animal that can run him off and save them.

Polly Hopper's Pouch by Louise Bonnett-Rampersaud, 2001. Polly wonders what her pouch is for until she has a baby Joey, who fits in it perfectly.

What Did You Put in Your Pocket? by Beatrice Schenk de Regniers, 2003. Kangaroo tells the other animals what he puts in his pocket each day.

When Kangaroo Goes to School by Sonia Levitin, 2001. Kangaroo shows all the things you do when you start to school including the proper way to behave.

Crafty Corner

Jumping Kangaroo

Materials: One rectangle-shaped piece of cardboard, blue and green construction paper, a hole-punch, and brown card stock.

Instructions:

1. Cut out a kangaroo shape from the brown card stock *(patterns on page 176)*.
2. Wrap green construction paper around your piece of cardboard, lined up with the bottom edge of the cardboard, and glue on. This will be your grass.
3. Wrap blue paper, slightly overlapping the green, with the edge even with the top side of the cardboard. This will be your sky.
4. By using a hole-punch, make a hole in the middle of the top and bottom of the cardboard.
5. Pull a piece of yarn through both holes and tie together on the back.
6. Glue or tape the kangaroo to the yarn at the front. Pull the string up and down from the back; the kangaroo will appear to jump up and down.

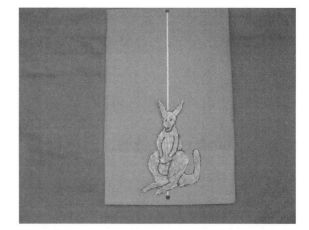

Figure 16-1. Jumping Kangaroo

Alternatives: Cut kangaroo from construction paper or craft foam. Use solid blue and green contact paper to cover the cardboard. Use a die-cut kangaroo shape instead of the provided pattern. For younger children, precut the kangaroo and punch the holes.

. . . PLUS

Games

Kangaroo Relays

Read the book *Jump, Kangaroo, Jump!* and have your own relay contests similar to the ones in the book and make up some of your own.

Longer Projects

For older school children, read the book *Too Many Kangaroo Things to Do* by Stuart J. Murphy, 1996, which is about animals getting ready for a birthday party. Create a math learning center. Set up a table with all the things that appear in the story (oranges, ribbons, birthday candles, cake mix, etc.). Take turns picking out what the animals get in the book, and then change things around with different instructions. Also use *Jump, Kangaroo, Jump!* and divide the kangaroos similar to the book by using felt, cards, or small toys.

Tell Aloud

Make a flannel board story from the book *I Love You, Blue Kangaroo*. Make the flannel story pieces for all the stuffed animals including Blue Kangaroo. For a smaller group, pass out the flannel animals to the children to bring them up to put on the flannel board.

Food

Make Kangaroo Pouches by pressing out biscuits; add onto the flattened biscuit things such as cheese, lunch meat, and veggies. Fold them over and bake according to the directions, and you have a surprise in a pouch. If you read the book *Too Many Kangaroo Things to Do,* bake a birthday cake together, or serve cupcakes.

Tips

The book *Marsupial Sue* by John Lithgow includes a CD with the rhyming text of the book put to music. Have a sing-along after reading the book about a kangaroo who dislikes being a kangaroo. Make a list of different types of marsupials.

Wear an apron or shirt with lots of pockets and put a kangaroo puppet and lots of other things in them. Let the children guess what some of the things are. Do this after reading *What Did You Put in Your Pocket?*

Read the books *Boing*; *Jump, Kangaroo, Jump!* and *McGillycuddy Could!* and talk about the importance of not giving up but continuing to try when you are at first not good at something.

Program 17

LIZARD'S SONG

Enjoy stories about lizards as they sing about their homes, hunt for their tails, make friends, and have many adventures. Little chameleons, who have problems with changing their color, come to realize they are fine the way they are.

Storytimes . . .

1. Rhymes and Songs

Five Little Lizards

Did You Ever See a Lizard?

I'm Bringing Home a Lizard

I'm a Little Chameleon

2. Storytime Picks

A Color of His Own by Leo Lionni

Do You Still Love Me? by Charlotte Middleton

Hide Clyde by Russell Benfanti

Izzy the Lizzy by Renee Riva

Leon the Chameleon by Melanie Watt

Lizard's Song by George Shannon

Lunchroom Lizard by Daniel Kirk

Where's My Tail? by Susan Schafer

3. Crafty Corner

Lizard's Home

. . . Plus

4. Games

Chameleon Beanbag Toss

5. Longer Projects

Lizard's Home Diorama

6. Tell Aloud

Lizard's Song

7. Food

Gummy Candy

8. Tips

STORYTIMES . . .

Rhymes and Songs

Five Little Lizards *(A Flannel Rhyme)*

Five little lizards all in a row.
What should they do and where should
    they go?
One little lizard was such a clever fellow.
He climbed onto a pretty flower,
and turned the color yellow.

Four little lizards all in a row.
What should they do and where should
    they go?
One little lizard did not want to be found.
He climbed onto a tree trunk,
and turned the color brown.

Three little lizards all in a row.
What should they do and where should
    they go?
One little lizard scooted underneath my bed.
He poked his little head out,
and he had turned the color red.

Two little lizards all in a row.
What should they do and where should
    they go?
One little lizard was very very bold.
He climbed onto a pile of hay,
and turned the color gold.

One little lizard standing all alone.
What should he do and where should he go?
That last little lizard climbed on my dog Spot.
And that little lizard turned a funny
    polka-dot.

Did You Ever See a Lizard?

Tune: Did You Ever See a Lassie

Did you ever see a lizard, a lizard, a lizard?
Did you ever see a lizard stick out his long
    tongue?
This way, *(tongue in and out)* and that way,
    and this way, and that way.
Did you ever see a lizard stick out his long
    tongue?

Did you ever see a lizard, a lizard, a lizard?
Did you ever see a lizard climb up a steep
    wall?
(Make climbing motions)
Climb up a steep wall, steep wall, steep wall,
Did you ever see a lizard climb up a steep
    wall?

Did you ever see a lizard, a lizard, a lizard?
Did you ever see a lizard curl up his long
    tail?
Curl up his long tail, his tail, yes his tail?
    (Twirl)
Did you ever see a lizard curl up his long
    tail?

Did you ever see a lizard, a lizard, a lizard?
Did you ever see a lizard run this way and
    that?

Run this way and that way, and this way and
    that way. *(Scoot left and right)*
Did you ever see a lizard run this way and
    that?

I'm Bringing Home a Lizard (*A Chameleon Song*)

Tune: I'm Bringing Home a Baby Bumblebee

Oh, I'm bringing home a lizard for my
    mom.
I put him on the yellow chair but now he's
    gone.
Hey, that silly little lizard got away from me.
Now, where could he be? *(Spoken)*
(Repeat the song, using other colors)

I'm a Little Chameleon

Tune: I'm a Little Teapot

I'm a little chameleon; I can be orange or
    green.
Or any color that you have ever seen.
Put me by something, and I will change for
    you.
To brown, red, purple, yellow, black, or
    blue.

Storytime Picks

A Color of His Own by Leo Lionni, 1994. A chameleon is tired of changing colors and wants a special color of his own.

Do You Still Love Me? by Charlotte Middleton, 2003. Dudley the dog is jealous of the new pet lizard.

Hide Clyde by Russell Benfanti, 2002. The story of a chameleon that has trouble changing his skin to match the environment.

Izzy the Lizzy by Renee Riva, 2005. Izzy makes friends with a bee and a spider, and they all learn about showing mercy to one another.

Leon the Chameleon by Melanie Watt, 2001. Leon always stands out because he turns the wrong color.

Lizard's Song by George Shannon, 1992. Bear wants Lizard's song for his very own, and tries to take it from him.

Lunchroom Lizard by Daniel Kirk, 2004. A classroom pet lizard escapes and goes all around the school trying to catch a fly. In the same manner of the *I Spy* books, the lizard is featured in every picture for you to try to spot.

Where's My Tail? by Susan Schafer, 2005. A little lizard loses his tail after having a close call when chased by a bobcat. He doesn't know that lizards' tails grow back, so he sets out to look for his tail.

Crafty Corner

Lizard's Home

Materials: A paper plate, gray or brown spray paint, green craft foam, wiggle eyes, and a short piece of red yarn.

Instructions:

1. Prepaint the paper plates so they will be dry for the craft.
2. Cut a lizard shape from the craft foam *(patterns on page 177)*.
3. Glue or tape the yarn to the underside of the lizard's mouth for his tongue.
4. Add wiggle eyes, and glue the lizard to the paper plate.

Alternatives: Use green or white card stock or construction paper instead of craft foam. Children can color their rock with markers or crayons. Use die-cut lizard shapes instead of one from the pattern.

Figure 17-1. Lizard's Home

. . . PLUS

Games

Chameleon Beanbag Toss

Run off copies of the lizard *(patterns on page 177)* on plain paper or card stock so the lizard can be colored with crayons or markers. Print the names of many different colors on pieces card stock or construction paper, and turn them face down on the floor so the children do not see what color is on them. The children then toss several beanbags and turn over what they land on. Give them crayons or markers that are the same colors as the colors that their beanbags landed on. They can then create a chameleon with those colors using any pattern they want. Vote on the best design or color scheme.

Longer Projects

Create a diorama of the lizard's home. For the rock, make homemade play dough or use store-bought play dough and mix the colors to turn into a grayish rock color. Make the shape of the rock, and place it in a shoebox or plastic container, lining the bottom with sand for the ground. Put a small plastic lizard toy or model on top, and add other things as you wish to make the scene more realistic (leaves, twigs, other animals, etc.). Recipes for homemade play dough are easily available on the Internet or in craft books.

Children can help paint the paper plates for the lizard craft. Make sure they use markers or acrylic paint instead of spray paint.

Tell Aloud

Tell the story from the book *Lizard's Song* using props. This is a great tell-aloud book. Use a puppet or Beanie Baby for the lizard, and find a flat rock for the lizard to sit on for his home. Use a larger bear puppet or stuffed animal, and have the children sing along each time you sing the song from the book.

Food

Give out packages of gummy worms or bugs, so the children can eat food like a lizard does.

Tips

Make flannel lizards and chairs for the rhyme *Five Little Lizards (patterns on page 177)*. Make two sets of the lizards, one set green and the other set to match the color of the chairs. Glue the lizards together so you only need to flip them over when their color changes in the rhyme. Just add two dots for eyes, instead of wiggle eyes, so they will stick and flip easily.

Bring a lizard or gecko to class and place it in an aquarium, so the children can watch the behavior of a live lizard. Read *Lunchroom Lizard* and *Where's My Tail*.

For a storytime just on Chameleons, use the books *A Color of His Own, Hide Clyde*, and *Leon the Chameleon* by Watt. Add the songs and rhymes that are specifically about Chameleons and end with the Create a Chameleon Beanbag Toss Game.

Program 18

MIXED UP

What a mixed-up time you'll have with these crazy mixed-up adventures. Some animals are mixed up about where they are supposed to live and what to do; others long to be different and have body parts they admire from other animals, while others are brand new creations.

Storytimes . . .

1. Rhymes and Songs

The Mixed-Up Chameleon

They're Noisy, Noisy

The Way You Are

2. Storytime Picks

Cock-a-Doodle Moooo! A Mixed-Up Menagerie by Keith DuQuette

Just the Way You Are by Marcus Pfister

Mixed Beasts by Kenyon Cox

The Mixed-Up Chameleon by Eric Carle

Moo Who? by Margie Palatini

Oh, Crumps! by Lee Bock

There's a Cow in the Cabbage Patch by Clare Beaton

3. Crafty Corner

Mixed-Up Puzzles

. . . Plus

4. Games

Mix Up

5. Longer Projects

Mixed-Up Creature Center

Wall Drawing

6. Tell Aloud

The Mixed-Up Chameleon

The Six Foolish Fishermen

7. Food

Mixed-Up Pudding

8. Tips

STORYTIMES . . .

Rhymes and Songs

The Mixed-Up Chameleon

Tune: Itsy Bitsy Spider

The tiny little chameleon visited at the zoo.
He saw himself so slow, so weak, that he felt very blue.
He saw polar bear and thought "I wished I was like you."
And suddenly before your eyes, this very wish came true.
(Speaking) But was he happy?
No!
(Repeat verse, changing polar bear to

flamingo, fox, fish, deer, giraffe, turtle, elephant, seal, people)

The tiny little chameleon visited at the zoo.
He saw himself so all mixed up that he felt very blue.
He could not catch a fly to eat, and suddenly he knew.
That it's best to be what one is born, and to yourself be true.
(Speaking) Now was he happy?
Yes!

They're Noisy, Noisy

Tune: Shortnin' Bread

The goats are loose, they're noisy, noisy.
The goats are loose, they're mixed up now.

The farmer chases them back to the goat
pen,
back to the goat pen, the goat pen now.

The dogs are loose, they're noisy, noisy.
The dogs are loose, they're mixed up now.
The farmer chases them back to the hayloft,
back to the hayloft, the hayloft now.

The cows are loose, they're noisy, noisy.
The cows are loose, they're mixed up now.
The farmer chases them back to their
stalls,
back to their stalls, the barn stalls now.

The tomcats are loose, they're noisy, noisy.
The tomcats are loose, they're mixed up now.
The farmer can't catch those noisy tomcats.
Now all the animals are waking up now.

All the animals are back, are back in their
places.

All the animals are back, in their places
now.
But the farmer just stays up, stays up,
stays up.
The farmer just stays up, it's morning now.

The Way You Are

Tune: London Bridge

I like you the way you are,
the way you are,
the way you are.
I like you the way you are,
Don't you change.

I like me the way I am too,
I am too, I am too.
I like me the way I am too,
I won't change me.

Storytime Picks

Cock-a-Doodle Moooo! A Mixed-Up Menagerie by Keith DuQuette, 2004. Told in rhyme, this book describes both mythological creatures and other new creations that combine two different animals.

Just the Way You Are by Marcus Pfister, 2002. All the animals going to the party think they would be better off if something about them were changed. At the party, they find they are the best just the way they are, and they feel good when others admire traits that they have.

Mixed Beasts by Kenyon Cox, 2005. This book features pictures of mixed-up animals both mythological and made up.

The Mixed-Up Chameleon by Eric Carle, 1984. A chameleon wishes to have different parts from other animals but finds at the end he prefers to be himself.

Moo Who? by Margie Palatini, 2004. Hildra the cow gets hit on the head and loses her moo. The other animals on the farm try to help her remember her moo.

Oh, Crumps! by Lee Bock, 2003. A bilingual text about a farmer who tries to get a good night's sleep but keeps getting awakened by the animals and gets more and more confused as he describes what he has to do the next day.

There's a Cow in the Cabbage Patch by Clare Beaton, 2001. The animals on the farm are all in the wrong places and the farmer must find a way to get them back to where they belong.

Crafty Corner

Mixed-Up Puzzles

Materials: A precut blank puzzle and colored markers or crayons.

Instructions:

1. Give the children a blank puzzle and the markers or crayons so they can draw a creature of their own creation, or draw one from the stories.

2. Now mix up the puzzle by separating the pieces. The children can work their own puzzle and take turns with others working each other's puzzles.

Alternatives: For younger children, use larger puzzle pieces. If you have a puzzle die cut, first draw the picture on cardboard or card stock and then cut it.

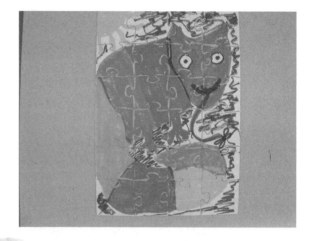

Figure 18-1. Mixed-Up Puzzles

. . . PLUS

Games

Mix Up
Start off with everyone standing in the middle of the room, and then let someone shout, "Mix up!" At this point everyone runs to one of several designated places that are numbered. Then choose one of the designated places by throwing a die, using a spinner, or drawing a number. The children who are in that particular place are out.

Longer Projects

Create a Mixed-Up Creature Center by putting out a variety of craft material (pom-poms, glitter, beads, feathers, wiggle eyes, wood shapes, pipe cleaners, markers, and glue). Children then create their own mixed-up, crazy, brand new animal. They can write a short story about their new imaginary animal telling about its name and characteristics, what it eats, where it lives, and so on. Have the children vote on their favorite creation.

Figure 18-2. Mixed-Up Creatures (Mixed-Up Center Example)

Put a large piece of butcher or similar paper on the wall. The first child will go up to the paper and with a marker will draw the head of any type of creature, real or imaginary. The next child will add one more body part (torso, ears, or some other part), and each child afterward will add another body part. See what your creature will turn into.

Tell Aloud

Instead of just reading the book, make large flannel pieces of the chameleon and the different body parts and tell the story from the book *The Mixed-Up Chameleon*. Let children add the flannel parts as the story goes along. Make a few extra parts, and go beyond the book by changing the chameleon with things from a few other creatures.

Tell the story of *The Six Foolish Fishermen*. This is a tale of six brothers who each thinks one brother has drowned because when they counted each other, they each forgot to count themselves. Use the children to point as you count, and show how the brothers got mixed up. Several book versions are available for this tale, including one by Robert D. San Souci.

Food

Serve mixed-up pudding by buying pudding cups that swirl two different types of pudding together, or make your own. You might also make a cake or cupcakes that have both vanilla and chocolate swirled together.

Tips

Older children will enjoy reading *Jackalope* by Janet Stevens, 2003, a Texas tall-tale about a rabbit that doesn't want to be ordinary and so wishes to have horns like a longhorn cow does. Find out what happens when his Fairy God Rabbit gives him his wish.

Another good choice for older children is the book **No Such Things** by Bill Peet. This a colorful collection of very unusual and funny mixed-up creatures, in which one is called "The No Such Thing Creature" and has backward feet.

For a mixed-up farm theme, combine the books **Moo Who?**, **Oh, Crumps!**, and **There's a Cow in the Cabbage Patch** with the song **They're Noisy, Noisy**. The song was written to go with the animals in **Oh, Crumps!** but you can add other farm animals to it such as a pig, chickens, and so on.

Combine the song **The Mixed-Up Chameleon** with the book **The Mixed-Up Chameleon** by Eric Carle. The song was written to go with that book.

Program 19

MUSHY MUD

Who doesn't love playing in the mud? Share the adventures of pigs, ducks, dogs, and children frolicking in the mud, playing and making marvelous mud pies.

Storytimes . . .

1. Rhymes and Songs

Wading in the Mud

Mud, Mud, Mud

Little Raindrops

2. Storytime Picks

Best Mud Pie by Lin Quinn

Bubba and Beau Meet the Relatives by Kathi Appelt

Ducks in Muck by Lois Haskins

Mud by Mary Lyn Ray

Mud by Charnan Simon

Pigs in Mud in the Middle of the Road by Lynn Plourde

Preschool to the Rescue by Judy Sierra

3. Crafty Corner

Muddy Animal Finger Puppets

. . . Plus

4. Games

Tracking Mud

5. Longer Projects

Ant Farm

Making Mud

6. Tell Aloud

Harry the Dirty Dog

7. Food

Dirt Pudding

8. Tips

STORYTIMES . . .

Rhymes and Songs

Wading in Mud

Tune: She Waded in the Water

I waded in the mud until I got my toes all muddy. *(Point)*
I waded in the mud until I got my toes all muddy.
I waded in the mud until I got my toes all muddy.
But I didn't get my clothes a mess *(clap)* yet.

Additional verses:
I waded in the mud until I got my ankles muddy . . .
I waded in the mud until I got my knees all muddy . . .

I waded in the mud until I got my hands all muddy . . .
I waded in the mud until I got my legs all muddy . . .

Final verse:
I waded in the mud until I fell into the mess. *(Dip down)*
I waded in the mud until I fell into the mess.
I waded in the mud until I fell into the mess.
And now my clothes are a mess *(clap)*.
Yes!

Mud, Mud, Mud

Tune: Skip to My Lou

Mud, mud, mud on my left *(Point left)*
Mud, mud, mud on my right. *(Point right)*
Mud, mud, every place. *(Look or point all around)*

It's been raining all morning. *(Fingers as rain)*

Mud, mud, mud on my toes. *(Repeat motions)*
Mud, mud, mud on my nose.
Mud, mud every place.
It's been raining all morning.

Mud, mud, mud on my knees. *(Repeat motions)*
Mud, mud, mud on my face.
Mud, mud, mud every place.
It's been raining all morning.

Little Raindrops

Tune: Ten Little Indians

One little, two little, three little raindrops
Four little, five little, six little raindrops

Seven, eight, nine, and ten little raindrops
Rain is falling from the sky.

Rain is making the road all muddy.
Rain is making the road all muddy.
Rain is making the road all muddy.
Rain is falling from the sky.

We'll take big steps and wear our rain boots.
We'll take big steps and wear our rain boots.
We'll take big steps and wear our rain boots.
Rain is falling from the sky.

After school, we'll go make mud pies.
After school, we'll go make mud pies.
After school, we'll go make mud pies.
Rain is falling from the sky.

One little, two little, three little raindrops
Four little, five little, six little raindrops
Seven, eight, nine, and ten little raindrops
Rain is falling from the sky.

Storytime Picks

Best Mud Pie by Lin Quinn, 2002. Roberto shows how to make mud pies with a secret recipe that he won't share with anyone.

Bubba and Beau Meet the Relatives by Kathi Appelt, 2004. Bubba and his dog Beau want to play in the mud, but the relatives are coming to visit, and his parents want him to be clean.

Ducks in Muck by Lois Haskins, 2000. Ducks are stuck in the mud. When the farmer puts the ducks in cages, he gets stuck too.

Mud by Mary Lyn Ray, 2001. A story about spring rain, and with the rain comes the mud.

Mud by Charnan Simon, 1999. Real pictures with simple words show a trio of boys who go out to play in the mud.

Pigs in Mud in the Middle of the Road by Lynn Plourde, 1997. Told in rhyme, first the pigs block the muddy road, then all the other animals, until Grandma comes to the rescue.

Preschool to the Rescue by Judy Sierra, 2001. A deep mud hole swallows a pizza van, a police car, and more until a group of preschoolers come to their rescue.

Crafty Corner

Muddy Animal Finger Puppets

Materials: Felt pieces in various colors, wiggle eyes, a marker, and craft glue.

Instructions:

1. Cut out two identical pieces for each animal *(patterns on page 178)*.

2. Glue the two matching pieces together around the top and sides only, leaving the bottom unglued so it will be open for a finger to fit into the finished puppet.

3. For the pig, glue on the nose, draw two dots on the nose for the nostrils, and add wiggle eyes.

4. For the duck, glue down half of the beak and fold it over, and add the wiggle eyes.

5. For the dog, add one wiggle eye since the dog is in profile, and draw on a mouth. For

a dog like Harry, use white flannel and the pointed ears and nose, and rub on a bit of marker for dirt. For a dog like Beau, use brown flannel, long ears, a rounder nose, and a few freckles.

Alternatives: Make a large brown flannel mud puddle so the puppets can roll in the mud. Create other types of dogs by interchanging the pattern piece and flannel colors. Make only the animals you wish, or create a new one. Use die cuts instead of the patterns.

Figure 19-1. Muddy Animal Finger Puppets

. . . PLUS

Games

Tracking Mud

Cut and laminate large footprint shapes out of different colors of construction paper or card stock (make several brown ones). Spread them on the floor in a large circle; put one footprint for each child playing (double-stick tape will keep them in place). Play music while children walk around stepping only on the footprints. When you stop the music, the children must stop where they are, and those standing on brown footprints have "tracked mud" and so must leave the circle to wash their feet.

Longer Projects

Bring an ant farm, and the children can observe an ant's activities within the dirt. Sing and march to the song *The Ants Go Marching One by One*.

Play in the mud, but substitute sand instead. Put the sand in a plastic swimming pool. Instead of playing in sand or mud, try this fun substitute: Blend 2 cups of sand and 1 cup cornstarch to 1 cup water. Increase the recipe as needed. Put the mixture in a large bowl, and see how it changes from hard to liquid.

Tell Aloud

Make a flannel story from an old favorite, *Harry the Dirty Dog* by Gene Zion. Harry the little white dog with black spots hates baths so much he runs away and becomes a little black dog with white spots, and his owners don't recognize him. Make flannel stick puppets to go with the story *(patterns on page 178)*.

Tell the story of *Ducks in Muck* by turning it into a flannel board story. Make a large flannel mud hole from brown flannel, and make the animals to go with the story. Let the children put the animal flannel pieces into the mud hole to get stuck.

Food

Make Dirt Pudding (or Mud Pudding) by filling a bowl or individual cups with chocolate pudding, or use instant premade pudding cups. Decorate the top of the pudding with crushed Oreo cookies and gummy worms.

Tips

Read **Pigs in Mud in the Middle of the Road,** and have the children act out the critters and the family members. Place a large piece of brown paper, material, or a rug on the floor to be the mud hole, large enough for everyone to end up standing on by the end of the book.

Schoolchildren will enjoy the story of **Golem** by Davis Wisnieski, the 1997 Caldecott medal winner. This is a picture book based on a Jewish legend of a monster made from mud.

Program 20

PANCAKE DAY

What better treat in the morning than to wake up to pancakes? Learn how to make pancakes, and hear stories from pancakes running away to tales of many different animals who love to eat them.

Storytimes . . .

1. Rhymes and Songs

Pancake Man

Let's Cook a Pancake

Ten Little Pancakes

2. Storytime Picks

Curious George Makes Pancakes by Margaret Rey

The Great Pancake Escape by Paul Many

Hey, Pancakes! by Tamson Weston

If You Give a Pig a Pancake by Laura Joffe Numeroff

One Hundred Pancakes by Keith Baker

Pancakes, Pancakes by Eric Carle

3. Crafty Corner

Skillet and Pancake

Pancake Man

. . . Plus

4. Games

Pancake Race

5. Longer Projects

Painting

Pancake Math Center

6. Tell Aloud

The Pancake Man

Have You Seen the Pancake Man?

The Runaway Pancake

7. Food

Pancakes

8. Tips

STORYTIMES . . .

Rhymes and Songs

Pancake Man (*A Rhyme*)

Early one morning, Mom got out her pan.
She mixed and she stirred, and made a pancake man.
She got out the butter and the sticky syrup too.
And down the stairs my brother quickly flew.

Early one morning, Mom got out her pan.
She mixed and she stirred, and made a pancake man.
And when she put the pancakes onto a plate,
My sister hurried down so she wouldn't be late.

Early one morning, Mom got out her pan.

She mixed and she stirred, and made a pancake man.
My dad smelled the pancakes, and he began to run.
He hurried down the stairs so he'd surely get him one.

Early one morning, Mom got out her pan.
She mixed and she stirred, and made a pancake man.
Everyone is sitting here, happy as can be
Now who's running down the stairs?
(*Point to self*) Me!

Let's Cook a Pancake

Tune: The Bear Went Over the Mountain

Oh, let's cook a pancake.
Oh, let's cook a pancake.
Oh, let's cook a pancake.
Let's cook it in a pan.

Let's mix it up and pour it.
Let's mix it up and pour it.
Let's mix it up and pour it.
Let's pour it in the pan.

The pancake is starting to bubble.
The pancake is starting to bubble.
The pancake is starting to bubble.
As it cooks inside the pan.

Now it's time to flip it.
Now it's time to flip it.
Now it's time to flip it.
Flip it over in the pan.

Let's eat it with butter and syrup.
Let's eat it with butter and syrup.

Let's eat it with butter and syrup.
Let's eat it as fast as we can.

Ten Little Pancakes

Tune: Ten Little Indians

One little, two little, three little pancakes.
Four little, five little, six little pancakes.
Seven, eight, nine little, ten little pancakes.
Piled up on my plate *(Hands showing tall)*

Ten little, nine little, eight little pancakes.
Seven little, six little, five little pancakes.
Four, three, two and one little pancake.
They all went down just great *(Pat tummy)*

Storytime Picks

Curious George Makes Pancakes by Margaret Rey, 1998. A mischievous monkey learns to make pancakes and is a big hit at the pancake benefit.

The Great Pancake Escape by Paul Many, 2002. Dad, who is a magician, bungles a spell while making breakfast, and the pancakes go wild.

Hey, Pancakes! by Tamson Weston, 2003. Three children wake up and make pancakes for breakfast.

If You Give a Pig a Pancake by Laura Joffe Numeroff, 1998. If you give a pig a pancake, then pig will want some syrup to go with it, and then he'll keep wanting more and more.

One Hundred Pancakes from the book *Meet Mr. and Mrs. Green* by Keith Baker, 2004. Mr. Green, an alligator, wants Mrs. Green to make him 100 pancakes for breakfast.

Pancakes, Pancakes by Eric Carle, 1998. Jack shows the process of how pancakes are made, starting all the way back to gathering the eggs from the hen house, the milk from the cow, and so on.

Crafty Corner

Skillet and Pancake

Materials: Paper plates, yellow or brown sponge sheets, wooden rulers, gray and black paint.

Instructions:

1. Paint or color the paper plates gray or silver to look like a pan and the wooden ruler black for the handle.
2. Cut the sponges into circle shapes to resemble a pancake. Wet the sponges after cutting and then let them dry.
3. Glue the ruler to the bottom of the paper plate for the handle of the pan.

Alternatives: Use a paint stick or large popsicle stick instead of a ruler for the handle. For younger children, paint the plates and handles in advance.

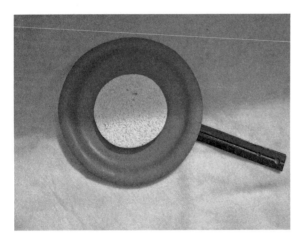

Figure 20-1. Skillet and Pancake

Pancake Man

Materials: Tan or yellow craft foam, pipe cleaners, wiggle eyes, and a popsicle stick.

Instructions:

1. Cut circle shapes out of the craft foam. Use something round to trace the circle before cutting.

2. Tape or glue one pipe cleaner to the back of the dry sponge for the arms and another for the legs. Bend the ends to make feet and hands.

3. Add the wiggle eyes and draw a mouth. Glue a popsicle stick to the back.

Alternatives: Use card stock, sponges, or construction paper for the pancake. Instead of a popsicle stick, use a magnet or a string so you can hang it up.

Figure 20-2. Pancake Man

. . . PLUS

Games

Pancake Race
Using the skillet and pancake from the craft, have a relay race. See who can carry the pancakes the fastest without dropping them, toss the pancakes in the air and see who can toss their pancake the highest, or try tossing the pancakes back and forth to each other.

Longer Projects

Older children can help prepare the paper plates and sponges for the craft by painting them with acrylic or coloring them with crayons or markers. They can also cut out the sponges and dip them in water. Supplement a lesson on sea life with sponges.

For school-age children make pancakes from sponges, foam, or card stock to create a Pancake Math Center. Add the book **One Hundred Pancakes** so they can count with Mr. and Mrs. Green and the book **Pancakes, Pancakes** so children can practice writing out the steps of making pancakes.

Tell Aloud

The Best of Totline Flannelboards by Totline contains two pancake flannel stories, **The Pancake Man** (page 100) and **Have You Seen the Pancake Man?** (page 101). Another good story for telling aloud or flannel is **The Runaway Pancake** (available in several versions).

Food

Make pancakes from scratch, or use frozen pancakes. Decorate them with fruit or just leave them plain. Make a face on the pancake with the fruit.

Tips

While doing the rhyme *Pancake Man* and the song *Let's Cook a Pancake,* use props and act out the words of the rhyme. It is also fun to use the pancake man from the craft to hold up as the pancake man is mentioned.

Older children will enjoy the humorous version of *The Little Red Hen* in the book **Mr. Wolf's Pancakes** by Jan Fearnley. The nice and polite wolf is making pancakes and everyone he asks to help him is rude because he is a wolf, so he has to do everything himself. When he finishes his pancakes, the wolf eats all the pancakes himself, and also eats everyone who wouldn't help him.

If you prepare the sponges in advance, demonstrate how the sponges start out flat and poof out when they are put into water.

Program 21

PEEK-A-BOO

It's always fun to play peek-a-boo and hide and seek. Share stories about little animals that play these games at the zoo and at the farm and of children playfully hiding from their family members.

Storytimes . . .

1. Rhymes and Songs

Peek-a-Boo

Where Are You Hiding?

The Seeing Song

I'm Hiding

2. Storytime Picks

Daisy's Hide and Seek by Jane Simmons

Peek-a-boo at the Zoo by Frank B. Edwards

Toby, Where Are You? by William Steig

Where Is Maisy? by Lucy Cousins

Where, Oh Where, Is Kipper's Bear? by Mike Inkpen

Where's Spot? by Eric Hill

3. Crafty Corner

Peek-a-Boo Animals or Aliens

. . . Plus

4. Games

Hide and Seek Me!

Where Is It?

5. Longer Projects

Surprise Garden

Painting

6. Tell Aloud

Three Billy Goats Gruff

Sodysallyrytus

The Elves and the Shoemakers

Jack and the Beanstalk

7. Food

Surprise Inside Treat

8. Tips

STORYTIMES . . .

Rhymes and Songs

Peek-a-Boo (*A Rhyme*)

(*When saying peek-a-boo cover your face and open your hands*)
Five little children were hiding behind the door.
One jumped up, said "Peek-a-boo!"
And then there were four.

Four little children were hiding behind the tree.
One jumped up, said "Peek-a-boo!"
And then there were three.

Three little children were behind a door of blue.
One jumped up, said "Peek-a-boo!"

And then there were two.

Two little children waiting to have some fun.
One jumped up, said "Peek-a-boo!"
And then there was one.

One little child was standing all alone.
There's no one left to "Peek-a-boo,"
so he went home.

Where Are You Hiding?

Tune: Frere Jacques

Where are you hiding? Where are you hiding? (*Look around*)
I'm looking for you. I'm looking for you. (*Point*)
I am going to find you. I am going to find you.

Peek-a-boo! Peek-a-boo!
(Cover eyes with your hands and peek-a-boo)

Where are you hiding? Where are you hiding?
There you are. *(Point)* There you are.
I'm so glad to see you. I'm so glad to see you.
Peek-a-boo! Peek-a-boo!

Now it's my turn. Now it's my turn. *(Point to self)*
You look for me. You look for me.
Find where I am hiding. Find where I am hiding.
Peek-a-boo! Peek-a-boo!

The Seeing Song

Tune: I Love You, You Love Me

I see you. You see me.
What are all the things that we can see?
When I look up and down, and all around the room, *(Look around)*
Tell me things that you see too.

I'm Hiding

Turn: It's Raining, It's Pouring

I'm hiding, I'm hiding,
Oh won't you come and find me.
You'll look here, and you'll look there. *(Point)*
But I don't think you'll find me. *(Shake finger)*

I'm hiding, I'm hiding,
Oh won't you come and find me.
You'll look under this, and over that. *(Point)*
But I don't think you'll find me. *(Shake finger)*

I'm hiding, I'm hiding,
Oh won't you come and find me.
I'll look inside here, and all around,
But I don't think you'll find me.

Storytime Picks

Daisy's Hide and Seek by Jane Simmons, 2001. A lift-the-flap book shows Daisy the duck and her little brother Pip playing hide and seek.

Peek-a-boo at the Zoo by Frank B. Edwards, 1999. A visitor to the zoo looks for the animals behind the rocks and trees.

Toby, Where Are You? by William Steig, 1997. Toby hides from his parents. Try to spot Toby as his parents look for him.

Where Is Maisy? by Lucy Cousins, 1999. Maisy the mouse is playing hide and seek, and you can help to find her.

Where, Oh Where, Is Kipper's Bear? A Pop-up Book with Light by Mike Inkpen, 1995. It's time for bed, and Kipper the dog can't find his bear.

Where's Spot? by Eric Hill, 1980. Help Spot's mother find out where he is hiding by lifting the flaps.

Crafty Corner

Peek-a-Boo Animals or Aliens

Materials: Disposable cups, small die-cut animals from card stock or construction paper, popsicle sticks, pom-poms, pipe cleaners, wiggle eyes, and crayons or markers.

Instructions:

1. In advance, cut a slit in the bottom of the cup that will allow a popsicle stick to slide through easily. (Paper cups are easier to work with than plastic.)

2. Decorate the cup and sticks with crayons or markers, stickers, paper, or other items.

3. Decorate the cups (use zigzag green paper for grass, glitter, markers, stickers, etc.).

4. For a bunny, glue a die cut to the popsicle stick, add wiggle eyes and a small pom-pom nose, and draw whiskers.

5. For a pop-up alien, glue a medium-size pom-pom to the popsicle stick and add wiggle eyes, a small pom-pom nose, and pipe cleaner antennas.

6. Put both figures into the cups with the stick sliding through the slit so you can push the figures up and down.

Alternatives: Let the children create other types of animals or creatures. Use craft foam instead of card stock or construction paper for the animals. Buy precolored sticks if there is not time to color them.

Figure 21-1. Peek-a-Boo Animals or Aliens

. . . PLUS

Games

Hide and Seek Me!

In this game, similar to the traditional game of Marco-Polo, but on dry land, one child hunts for others while blindfolded or with eyes shut. The blindfolded child will call out the word "Hide," and then all the others must call the words "Seek me" each time. The blindfolded child tries to find the others by following the sound of their voices.

Alternatives: Play traditional hide and seek, or hide stuffed animals or puppets and have the children find them.

Where Is It?

School-age children will enjoy this concentration game. Line up several cups face down, and place a small object (such as a seed, rock, or ball) under one of them. Quickly slide the cups around and back and forth as fast as you can while the guesser watches and tries to keep up with which cup has the object, so they can guess where it is when the cups are still.

Longer Projects

Mix types of flower seeds, and give each child a small bag of seeds to take home and plant. Plant the seeds close by outside if you have an area, in a window box, or in a large flower pot. As the seeds grow, the children will have a surprise seeing what types of flowers come up.

Let older children paint the cups and sticks used for the craft with acrylic paint.

Tell Aloud

Tell a traditional folktale or flannel story that involves someone hiding. Several good ones are *Three Billy Goats Gruff, Sodysallyrytus, The Elves and the Shoemakers,* and *Jack and the Beanstalk.*

Food

Serve some type of treat that has a hidden surprise, such as a cupcake with cream inside, a sucker with a chocolate or bubblegum center, or oatmeal with dinosaur eggs that melt into candy dinosaurs; or give out plastic eggs with a surprise treat hidden inside.

Tips

Children will enjoy looking at *I Spy* or **Where's Waldo** books, which require you to find an object or objects hidden among the pictures on the page. For older children, try putting out books of optical illusions and 3-D image books.

Use the Peek-a-Boo Animal or Alien craft with the song **Where Are You Hiding?** and rhyme **Peek-a-Boo,** and pop the creatures up and shout during the peek-a-boo parts.

During the **Seeing Song**, place objects such as stuffed animals around the room, and then describe a particular item for the children to spot.

Program 22

PLENTY OF POCKETS

❦

What's in your pocket? Tell stories about all the things that are in the many pockets of children, teddy bears, and kangaroos, and see who can guess some of the many things that are inside.

Storytimes . . .	**. . . Plus**

Storytimes . . .

1. Rhymes and Songs

My Pockets

There's a Hole in My Pocket

Pockets, Pockets, What's Inside?

A Pocket, a Pocket

2. Storytime Picks

Empty Pockets by Faye Van Wert

Kathy's Pocket by Paul Harvey

A Pocket for Corduroy by Don Freeman

Six Empty Pockets by Matt Curtis

What Did You Put in Your Pocket? by Beatrice Schenk de Regniers

What's in My Pocket? A Pop-Up and Peek-In Book by David Carter

3. Crafty Corner

Teddy Bear with Pocket

. . . Plus

4. Games

Pocket Match

Pocket Guess

5. Longer Projects

Pocket Board

6. Tell Aloud

Katy No Pocket

7. Food

Pita Treat

8. Tips

❦

STORYTIMES . . .

Rhymes and Songs

My Pockets

Tune: Pawpaw Patch

I'm picking up shells and putting them in my
     pocket,
Picking up shells, and putting them in my
     pocket,
Picking up shells, and putting them in my
     pocket,
On the day we went to the shore and back.

Additional verses:
I'm picking up eggs and putting them in my
     pocket . . .
On the day we went to the farm and back.

I'm picking up flowers and putting them in
     my pocket . . .
On the day we went to the meadow and
     back.

I'm picking up rocks and putting them in my
     pocket . . .
On the day we went to the hills and back.

I'm picking up bugs and putting them in my
     pocket . . .
On the day we went to the pond and back.

There's a Hole in My Pocket

Tune: There's a Hole in My Bucket

There's a hole in my pocket,

my pocket, my pocket.
There's a hole in my pocket, my pocket, a
    hole!

I don't want to lose things,
to lose things, to lose things.
I don't want to lose things out of that
    hole.

I'll ask mom to sew it,
to sew it, to sew it.
I'll ask mom to sew it, to sew up that hole.

Now I won't lose things,
won't lose things, won't lose things.
Now I won't lose things out of that hole.

Pockets, Pockets, What's Inside?

Tune: Skip to My Lou

Pockets, pockets, what's inside?
Pockets, pockets, what's inside?
Pockets, pockets, what's inside?
Can you guess what's in here?

Pencil, pencil, a pencil is here.
Pencil, pencil, a pencil is here.
Pencil, pencil, a pencil is here.
A pencil's in my pocket.

Repeat with other things:
Watch, Watch, a watch is here . . .
A penny, a penny, a penny is here . . .
Comb, comb, a comb is here . . .

Last verse:
Pockets, pockets, what's inside?
Pockets, pockets, what's inside?
Pockets, pockets, what's inside?
Now my pockets are empty.

A Pocket, a Pocket

Tune: A Tisket, a Tasket

A pocket, a pocket
I see a great big pocket.
What will I see, hiding there
Inside that great big pocket?

Storytime Picks

Empty Pockets by Faye Van Wert, 2000. Stevie likes to collect all sorts of things and put them into his pockets.

Kathy's Pocket by Paul Harvey, 1994. A "Big Book" about Kathy the Kangaroo and what she puts in her pockets.

A Pocket for Corduroy by Don Freeman, 1980. The lovable bear Corduroy is back. When he goes to the Laundromat, he decides that he needs a pocket in his overalls.

Six Empty Pockets by Matt Curtis, 1998. Charles carries a variety of things in his six pockets.

What Did You Put in Your Pocket? by Beatrice Schenk de Regniers, 2003. Kangaroo tells the other animals what he puts in his pocket each day.

What's in My Pocket? A Pop-Up and Peek-In Book by David Carter, 1999. Lift the flap to find out what each animal has in its pocket and to find out what the animals like to eat.

Crafty Corner

Teddy Bear with Pocket

Materials: A large die-cut teddy bear, a piece of material for a pocket, wiggle eyes, a pom-pom for the nose, things to put in the pocket, and a marker.

Instructions:

1. Cut a piece of material in the shape of a pocket and glue it onto the bear, leaving the top open. (Precut this for younger children)

2. Glue on wiggle eyes and a pom-pom for the nose, and draw a smiling mouth.

3. Put something into the pocket.

Alternatives: Use a different animal instead of a bear. Draw a picture of Corduroy Bear instead of using a die-cut bear. Cut overalls from the material for the bear and glue a pocket on these. Glue the bear on a sheet of construction paper, or add a magnet on the back.

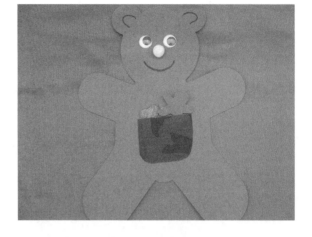

Figure 22-1. Teddy Bear with Pocket

. . . PLUS

Games

Pocket Match (A Memory Game)
Using blank index cards, glue a picture or place a sticker on one side, using two of each sticker or picture so there are two cards exactly the same. Put the cards in the pocket board that is described as follows, with the picture side turned in and not showing. Play by choosing two of the pockets by number, then turn over those cards. If they don't match, turn them back over, and if they do match, remove them and take another turn. The one with the most matches wins. (This can also be played by placing the cards flat on a table, but using them in a pocket ties the game to the theme.)

Pocket Guess
One person is selected to go first. That person gives one hint at a time about what he or she has in his or her pocket. Then the each group, team, or individual person can take one guess. The person who keeps everyone guessing the longest wins the game.

Longer Projects

Make a pocket board. Glue book pockets in rows to a sheet of poster board. The book pockets come in different colors, which will make your board more attractive, or have the children color and decorate manila or plain pockets. Make five rows of pockets across and five down. Use this for games, chore lists, sorting, grouping, or other activities. Decorate the pockets, if you wish, with lace, fabric, buttons, drawings, or other materials.

Tell Aloud

Make flannel board pieces to tell a flannel story, or use stuffed animals or puppets to tell the story **Katy No Pocket** by Emma Payne, illustrated by H. A. Rey, who created Curious George. Katy, a kangaroo without a pocket, asks other animals how they carry their own babies and through persistence finds a solution to her problem.

Food

Make a pocket sandwich using pita pocket bread, and stuff the inside with goodies such as peanut butter, grated cheese, sprouts, lettuce, or whatever things you like.

Tips

Have puppets or stuffed toys placed around the room. Use animals that have pockets, such as kangaroos, wallabies, koalas, or possums, or use toys or animals that have clothes on them with pockets, such as a Corduroy doll. Describe certain ones and let the children guess which one you are talking about.

Wear a shirt or apron that has a lot of pockets, and use it to hold props. Put in things that go with the songs *Pockets, Pockets, What's Inside?* and *My Pockets*.

Place some surprises in your pockets, sing the song *A Pocket, a Pocket*, and then let the children guess what the things are. Put in some unusual things and give them hints if needed.

Show the short video *A Pocket for Corduroy*, a live-action adaptation based on the book by Don Freeman.

Program 23

RAINBOW DAY

There are all kinds of rainbows, from rainbows seen in the sky after a rain, to beautiful rows of flowers, to the beautiful colors of nature. And if you happen to be lucky enough to catch a leprechaun, you might get a surprise at the end of a rainbow.

Storytimes . . .	**. . . Plus**
1. Rhymes and Songs	4. Games
Did You Ever See a Rainbow?	Color Seek
Rainbow Colors	5. Longer Projects
I See a Rainbow	Wall Rainbow
2. Storytime Picks	6. Tell Aloud
Duckie's Rainbow by Francis Barry	*The Little Old Lady and the Leprechaun*
Maisy's Rainbow Day by Lucy Cousins	*Mother Nature's Gift*
Planting a Rainbow by Lois Ehlert	7. Food
Rainbow Fish by Marcus Pfister	Rainbow Jell-O
A Rainbow of My Own by Don Freeman	8. Tips
What Makes a Rainbow? by Betty Ann Schwartz	
3. Crafty Corner	
Rainbow Banner	

STORYTIMES . . .

Rhymes and Songs

Did You Ever See a Rainbow?

Tune: Did You Ever See a Lassie?

Did you ever see a rainbow, a rainbow, a
  rainbow?
Did you ever see a rainbow up high in the
  sky?
There's purple and blue and yellow and green.
Did you ever see a rainbow, up high in the
  sky?

Did you ever see a rainbow, a rainbow, a
  rainbow?
Did you ever see a rainbow up high in the
  sky?

There's red and there's violet, and orange so
  bright.
Did you ever see a rainbow, up high in the
  sky?

Rainbow Colors

Tune: If You're Happy and You Know It

If you know the colors of the rainbow, step
  right up. *(Stomp each foot)*
If you know the colors of the rainbow, step
  right up.
If you know the colors of the rainbow, well
  just step right up and say so.
If you know the colors of the rainbow, step
  right up.

If you see the color red, just nod your head.
  (Nod)

If you see the color red, just nod your
  head.
If you see the color red, well just step up and
  nod your head.
If you see the color red, just nod your head.

If you see the color green, be a jumping
  bean. *(Jump up and down)*
If you see the color green, be a jumping bean.
If you see the color green, just step up and
  be a jumping bean.
If you see the color green, be a jumping
  bean.

If you see the color black, just hop right
  back. *(Hop backward)*
If you see the color black, just hop right back.
If you see the color black, well just step up
  and hop right back.
If you see the color black, just hop right back.

If you see the color yellow, act like Jell-O.
  (Shake all over)
If you see the color yellow, act like Jell-O.
If you see the color yellow, just step up and
  act like Jell-O.
If you see the color yellow, act like Jell-O.

If you see the color blue, just stomp your
  shoe. *(Stomp foot)*
If you see the color blue, just stomp your
  shoe.

If you see the color blue, well just step up
  and stomp your shoe.
If you see the color blue, just stomp your
  shoe.

If you see the color white, go fly a kite.
  (Hold hand up, as if flying kite)
If you see the color white, go fly a kite.
If you see the color white, just step up and
  fly a kite.
If you see the color white, go fly a kite.

If you see the color pink, give a wink. *(Wink)*
If you see the color pink, give a wink.
If you see the color pink, just step up and
  give a wink.
If you see the color pink, give a wink.

I See a Rainbow

Tune: Oh My Darling, Clementine

I see a rainbow, a pretty rainbow.
I see a rainbow in the sky.
Let's look at colors, pretty colors,
Let's look at colors, you and I.

I see a rainbow, a pretty rainbow.
I see a rainbow in the sky.
What's that color, that pretty color,
in the rainbow, up in the sky?

Storytime Picks

Duckie's Rainbow by Francis Barry, 2004. On her way home to her nest, Duckie finds all sorts of colors and a surprise rainbow at the end.

Maisy's Rainbow Day by Lucy Cousins, 2003. Maisy dreams of all the different colors as she snoozes in her bed.

Planting a Rainbow by Lois Ehlert, 1992. A mother and her child plant a variety of pretty flowers which look like the colors of a rainbow after they grow.

Rainbow Fish by Marcus Pfister, 1992. Rainbow Fish has beautiful shiny scales but is vain. He soon learns it's better to have friends than to be beautiful.

A Rainbow of My Own by Don Freeman, 1966. A boy who wants a rainbow imagines he has one of his very own.

What Makes a Rainbow? by Betty Ann Schwartz, 2000. Color ribbons show the different colors of a rainbow by adding a new ribbon with each turned page.

Crafty Corner

Rainbow Banner
  Materials: Paper plates, different colors of crepe paper rolls or tissue paper, large popsicle sticks, stickers, and markers or crayons.

Instructions:

1. If you are using paper that is not in rolls, cut it into about 1-inch strips. Use the different rainbow colors.
2. In advance, cut paper plates into four pieces. Each child will get ¼ of a paper plate.
3. Decorate the paper plate piece and stick, using things such as crayons, markers, glitter, paint, stickers, or other materials.
4. Glue or tape the tissue paper streamers to the rounded end of the paper plate and the stick to the pointed end.

Alternatives: Buy precolored popsicle sticks. Use other shapes for the banner such as a whole small plate or half of a plate instead of a quarter, or cut the plate into a shape. Use different materials such as card stock or craft foam.

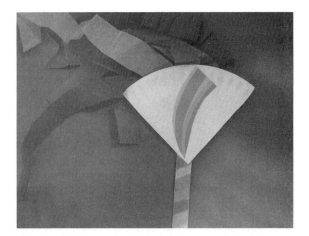

Figure 23-1. Rainbow Banner

. . . PLUS

Games

Color Seek

Ask children to spot items around the room with a particular color and point them out. Place things around the room, such as stuffed animals, toys, or knickknacks, that have a lot of colors in them, to make sure there are lots of things to spot. See which color is seen the most often and which is seen the least. Look for things that have several colors, polka dots, or stripes or that have a particular design.

Longer Projects

Create a large rainbow in the room by taping or stapling a large sheet of paper (such as butcher paper) on the wall. Take a pencil or marker and draw the shape of a rainbow. Let the children then dip their hands in finger paint and make handprints on the rainbow to add the color. For a less messy alternative, have them draw their hand shapes on different colors of paper, cut them out, and attach them to the rainbow.

Tell Aloud

Make a flannel from the story *The Little Old Lady and the Leprechaun* found in *Teeny-Tiny Folktales* by Jean Warren, page 54. This is a story of a little old lady who catches a leprechaun but is outsmarted by him. Make several of the flannel bushes and ribbons to put on them.

Make a flannel from *Mother Nature's Gift*, a Native American folktale about the first rainbow, adapted by Jean Warren and found in *Teeny-Tiny Folktales* on page 21.

There are four leprechaun flannel stories in *The Best of Totline Flannelboards* by Totline on pages 126–134.

Food

Serve Rainbow Jell-O by making Jell-O with several layers of different colors. You will need to put one layer in your dish or container, let it firm completely, and then add another. Top it with whipped topping and different colors of sprinkles.

Tips

When singing the song *I See a Rainbow,* hold up a picture of something with a particular color, or draw a wide mark on a sheet of paper using a marker or crayon. When you sing the part that asks, "What's That color?" have the children call out the color name. Repeat this with other colors.

Wear clothing that has many colors in it so you can point to the different colors as you sing the songs. Have children stand up or raise their hand if they are wearing the particular color.

Read *A Rainbow of My Own.* Then, using watercolors, have children paint a rainbow of their own on paper. If it's around Saint Patrick's Day, put on a sticker or glue on a picture of a pot of gold. Let each child take turns saying what they would like to find in their pot instead of gold.

Add a Saint Patrick's Day twist to your topic by reading the books *Jack and the Leprechaun* by Ivan Robertson or *Leprechaun Gold* by Teresa Bateman.

Program 24

READ TO ME

Who doesn't love to read and be read to? Enjoy stories of many animals that love books from the zoo to the barnyard to the pond, and share the adventures of children who learn what fun it is to go to the library.

Storytimes . . .

1. Rhymes and Songs

We Go to Storytime

The Reading Song

Five Little Books

I See a Book

2. Storytime Picks

Beatrice Doesn't Want To by Laura Numeroff

The Best Time to Read by Debbie Bertram

Book! Book! Book! by Deborah Bruss

I Took My Frog to the Library by Eric A. Kimmel

Maisy Goes to the Library by Lucy Cousins

Reading Makes You Feel Good by Todd Parr

Stella Louella's Runaway Book by Lisa Campbell Ernst

Wild About Books by Judy Sierra

3. Crafty Corner

Make Your Own Book

. . . Plus

4. Games

Guess Who?

Book Line-Up

5. Longer Projects

Reading Chart

Book-Making Center

6. Tell Aloud

Bubbadillo (See pages 158–159, 168)

The Frog Princess

7. Food

Graham Cracker Book

8. Tips

STORYTIMES . . .

Rhymes and Songs

We Go to Storytime

Tune: Wheels of the Bus

We go to storytime at the library,
At the library, at the library
We go to storytime at the library,
Anytime we can.

Repeat the song using the following:
We go to storytime to hear a story . . .
We go to storytime to sing a song . . .
We go to storytime to do a craft . . .
We go to storytime to say some rhymes . . .
We go to storytime and have lots of fun . . .

The Reading Song

Tune: Frere Jacques

I am learning, I am learning,
many things, many things.
My ABC's will teach me, my ABC's will
    teach me
how to read, how to read.

I know my letters, I know my letters.
Hear me read! Hear me read!
I'm ready to learn now; I'm ready to learn
    now.

Many things, many things.

When I'm reading, when I'm reading,
I will learn, I will learn,
Anything I want to, anything I want to,
anything, anything.

Let's go to the library, go to the library
To find a book, to find a book
I just love to read, I just love to read
All the time, all the time.

Five Little Books *(A Rhyme)*

Five little books just inside the library door,
One fell off the shelf, and then there were
    four.

Four little books hoping to be checked out
    by me,
One fell off the shelf, and then there were
    three.

Three little books hoping to be checked out
    by you,

One fell off the shelf, and then there were
    two.

Two little books hoping to give you some
    fun,
One fell off the shelf, and then there was
    one.

One little book standing all alone,
Let's pick them all up, and take them all
    home.
(Use flannel books of different colors)

I See a Book

Tune: Pop Goes the Weasel

I see a book upon the shelf. (Point up)
I'd really like to read it.
I'm climbing high, I'm reaching tall.
    (Stretch)
OOPS! (Sit down quickly)
Down I fall.

Storytime Picks

Beatrice Doesn't Want To by Laura Numeroff, 2004. Beatrice doesn't like going to the library with her brother until something changes her mind.

Best Time to Read by Debbie Bertram, 2005. A young boy wants to read, but no one has the time to listen to him.

Book! Book! Book! by Deborah Bruss, 2001. Barnyard animals make a visit to the library to get a book.

I Took My Frog to the Library by Eric A. Kimmel, 1992. When Bridgett brings her many pets to the library, it causes a ruckus.

Maisy Goes to the Library by Lucy Cousins, 2005. Maisy tells about the things that you can do at the library.

Reading Makes You Feel Good by Todd Parr, 2005. With bright colorful pictures, this book shows reasons why reading is enjoyable.

Stella Louella's Runaway Book by Lisa Campbell Ernst, 1998. Stella has misplaced her library book and her friends and neighbors help her find it.

Wild About Books by Judy Sierra, 2004. The librarian accidentally drives her bookmobile to the zoo, and the animals develop a love for reading.

Crafty Corner

Make Your Own Book

Materials: Sheets of any colored copy paper, a hole-punch, yarn, die cuts, and markers.

Instructions:

1. Fold several sheets of paper (sheets together) in half, lengthwise.

2. Cut the paper across the fold at the top. You will have a several sheets of long paper.

3. Fold the paper in the middle. This will give you the book.

4. Punch two holes at the end that has the fold, and run a piece of yarn through both holes and tie a bow at the front cover.

5. Let the children be creative in designing their book. Choose a theme or let the children pick one.

Alternatives: Depending on the age group you have, children can glue either die cuts or pictures on the pages, draw with markers or crayons, or write their own story and illustrate it. Staple the book instead of using ribbons, or do both. Cut pictures out of a magazine to put together to tell a story. For younger children, prepare the booklet in advance and give them the finished book to work with.

Figure 24-1. Make Your Own Book

. . . PLUS

Games

Guess Who?

Play a guessing game. Start by describing a character in a fairy tale or well-known story and see how long it takes for the children to guess the answer. Play in groups or individually. Once you demonstrate, let the children think of book characters or stories to guess.

Book Line-Up

Make a game that is similar to bingo. Take blank squares and fill them in using favorite stories, fairy tale or folktale characters, or library terms. Do a subject search for "Bingo Cards" and you will find several sites on making your own cards. Give schoolchildren a sheet with the squares empty, and have them fill in the squares with stickers or from a list of words that they can choose from. For younger children, hold up the pictures of the things you call out.

Longer Projects

Make a reading chart with each child's name and put on a sticker, star, or other decoration for each time the child reads a book or a certain amount of time. Have a prize or certificate when children reach a goal they have set for themselves.

For schoolchildren, create a center about book publishing and paper making. Learn the different steps involved in publishing from idea to book by reading books such as *I Am a Book* by Linda Hayward (2004) and *How a Book Is Made* by Aliki. Older grades might like to try paper making. Use instructions from books, or do a simple subject search on the Internet using the term "make paper" to find several sites with simple instructions available.

Homeschoolers or school classrooms can take a field trip to tour their public library or hear a storytime.

Tell Aloud

Present the puppet play *Bubbadillo (script on pages 158–159)*, written by Pat Snell. This is a story of a bored little armadillo who finds fun at his local library. If you wish, adapt the play to have Bubbadillo go to storytimes or to one of your own special programs.

Put on a play using the book *The Frog Princess* by Pamela Mann, a story of a little frog that claims to have read all the books the animals tell her about. They don't believe her until a prince comes along and the little frog turns out to be an enchanted librarian. The children can act out the different characters or use stick puppets or paper plate masks for the animals.

Food

Make an eatable book with graham cracker squares. Put marshmallows on a graham cracker, melt them slightly, and top with another graham cracker similar to a s'more. The marshmallow represents the pages between and the graham crackers the front and back cover of the book. Write a short title with icing (in a tube for writing), or just decorate the top with icing, candy bits or chips, or other edible decorations.

Tips

Make flannel books to use counting down with the rhyme *Five Little Books*, or use real books as props.

For an animals-who-love-books theme, combine: *Book! Book! Book!*, *I Took My Frog to the Library*, *Wild About Books*, and *The Frog Princess*, and make the craft book about the animals from the stories using dies cuts, drawings, or pictures.

Program 25

SHEARING SHEEP

Sheep can do a lot more than put you to sleep. You'll enjoy telling stories of sheep who drive, wear sweaters, and go to the library. And sometimes sheep need a little help falling asleep themselves.

Storytimes . . .

1. Rhymes and Songs

I'm a Little Sheep

Five Little Sheep

Shearing Sheep

2. Storytime Picks

Farmer Brown Shears His Sheep by Teri Sloat

Little Bo Peep's Library Book by Cressida Cowell

Sheep Asleep by Gloria Rothstein

Sheep Don't Count Sheep by Margaret Wise Brown

Sheep in a Jeep by Nancy Shaw

Ten Little Lambs by Alice B. McGinty

Where Is the Green Sheep? by Mem Fox

3. Crafty Corner

Fuzzy Sheep

. . . Plus

4. Games

Sheep Herding

Follow the Sheepherder

5. Longer Projects

Learn to Knit

Dye Cotton Balls

6. Tell Aloud

The Boy Who Cried Wolf

Flannel: *Mary's Lamb and Peter's Lamb*

7. Food

Cupcake Sheep

8. Tips

STORYTIMES . . .

Rhymes and Songs

I'm a Little Sheep

Tune: I'm a Little Teapot

I'm a little sheep so fat and furry. *(Motion hands wide)*
When Bo Peep starts looking, *(Look around)*
I run off in a hurry. *(Hop)*

But if she couldn't find me, I'd be alone.
(Look around)
So I wiggle my tail. *(Wiggle)*
And I head right home. *(Hop)*

Five Little Sheep (A Rhyme)

There were five little sheep in the meadow
one day. *(Hold up five fingers)*

One ran off because he wanted to play.
Well that farmer went looking, *(look around)* behind the barn door,
but now the little sheep was gone and there were only four.

There were four little sheep in the meadow
one day.
One ran off because he wanted to play.
Well the farmer went looking, he checked
behind the tree,
but that little sheep was gone and there were
only three.

There were three little sheep in the meadow
one day.
One ran off because he wanted to play.
Well the farmer went looking, behind a
truck of blue,
but that little sheep was gone and there were
only two.

There were two little sheep in the meadow
    one day.
One ran off because he wanted to play.
Well the farmer went looking and he started
    to run,
but that little sheep was gone and there was
    only one.

There was one little sheep in the meadow
    one day,
and that sheep ran off because he wanted to
    play.
Well the farmer went looking, but he was
    done,
since that last sheep was gone, now there
    were none.

There were no more sheep in the meadow
    that day.
They had all run off because they wanted to
    play.
But when the sun went down, and the day
    was gone,
those little sheep come back to sleep until
    the dawn.

Shearing Sheep

Tune: Itsy Bitsy Spider

The farmer sheared the sheep's wool,
early one spring day. *(Shearing
    motions)*

The sheep were so cold,
they did not know what to say.
    (Shiver)
The farmer washed the wool,
as they gathered and looked on.
But the sheep keep getting colder
since their fluffy coats were gone.

The farmer sheared the sheep's wool,
early one spring day. *(Shearing
    motions)*
The sheep were so cold,
they did not know what to say. *(Shiver)*
They carded, spun, and dyed it
to sell it by the pound.
Then sheep all looked for their wool,
but it was nowhere to be found.

The farmer sheared the sheep's wool,
early one spring day. *(Shearing motions)*
The sheep were so cold,
they did not know what to say. *(Shiver)*
The farmer filled his bags up
one by one. *(Motions of filling a bag)*
Then the farmer made them sweaters,
after he was done *(Pretend to knit)*

Storytime Picks

Farmer Brown Shears His Sheep by Teri Sloat, 2000. In this story, told in rhyme, Farmer Brown takes the sheep's wool through the different stages while it becomes yarn. Then later he makes sweaters for the cold sheep.

Little Bo Peep's Library Book by Cressida Cowell, 1999. Bo Peep has lost her sheep and goes to the library to find a book that will help her to find them.

Sheep Asleep by Gloria Rothstein, 2003. A delightful book in rhyme that counts down from ten, as the little sheep go to bed.

Sheep Don't Count Sheep by Margaret Wise Brown, 2003. The little sheep is having trouble falling asleep.

Sheep in a Jeep by Nancy Shaw, 1986. Five sheep make an ill-fated road trip and after much trouble get stuck in the mud.

Ten Little Lambs by Alice B. McGinty, 2002. In a counting rhyme, children dream of ten little lambs that go to sleep one by one.

Where Is the Green Sheep? by Mem Fox, 2004. Different colored sheep are doing many things, but no one knows where the green sheep is. This is good to use for opposites and colors.

Crafty Corner

Fuzzy Sheep

Materials: A die-cut sheep from white paper, colored cotton balls or fluffs, glue, magnets or popsicle sticks, and wiggle eyes.

Instructions:

1. Glue cotton balls to the sheep, leaving the face and legs uncovered so the cotton will look like sheep's wool.
2. Glue on a wiggle eye, and put the sheep on a magnet or popsicle stick.

Alternatives: If you don't use a die-cut sheep, draw your own, or use a pattern from a pattern book. Use white cotton balls on a sheep cut from black paper. Stock up on colored cotton balls at Easter.

Figure 25-1. Fuzzy Sheep

... PLUS

Games

Sheep Herding

Divide into at least two teams. Pick one child from each team for the sheepherder; the other children are the sheep. Blindfolded, one sheep will walk from one point to another, around obstacles (desks, chairs, etc.), by listening to the sheepherder call out directions on which way they should move. Once one sheep reaches the end, the next sheep goes. The first team to get all the sheep herded home wins.

Follow the Sheepherder

Play a game of follow the leader, and call the leader the sheepherder. The sheep will follow the sheepherder making the same motions and gestures as they go along.

Longer Projects

Older school grades will enjoy learning to knit or seeing a demonstration. If you know how, demonstrate this, or ask someone to visit and teach, or show a short how-to video.

Older schoolchildren can color their own cotton balls with food coloring. Dip the cotton balls in food coloring and water, squeeze slightly so they don't drip (don't squeeze out all the water), and let them dry completely. If they are not dark enough or the color is not even, dip them again. Make sure to wear gloves when handling the food coloring.

Tell Aloud

Tell or put on a play of the traditional story **The Boy Who Cried Wolf**. Talk about the lesson of the story.

The flannel **Mary's Lamb and Peter's Lamb** can be found on page 193 of the book **The Best of Totline Flannelboards** by Totline.

Food

Make a cupcake sheep by putting icing (any color) on a cupcake and adding a gumdrop or small marshmallow for the head and small dots of chocolate frosting for eyes. Add four short strips of thin licorice or small pretzel sticks to the sides for legs. Make the cupcakes with different colors of icing to match the sheep in the book *Farmer Brown Shears His Sheep*.

Tips

Read *Farmer Brown Shears His Sheep*, then say the song *Shearing Sheep* (it was written especially for this book) and finish up with the fuzzy sheep craft.

Use flannel sheep pieces as you count down while saying the rhyme *Five Little Sheep*. An alternative would be to make the sheep craft and have five (or more) children stand up in a row holding their sheep and drop their sheep as you count down.

For a sleepy sheep theme, read *Sheep Asleep*, *Sheep Don't Count Sheep*, and *Ten Little Lambs* and sing the song *I'm a Little Sheep*.

Combine the classic nursery rhyme and song *Little Bo Peep* and *Mary Had a Little Lamb* with the song *I'm a Little Sheep*, and then read the book *Baa, Baa, Black Sheep* by Iza Trapani.

Program 26

SNAIL TRAIL

What goes on in the world of a snail? Share stories of these little creatures as they go about their day, as they go on adventures and to school, and as they travel about the world leaving a trail behind.

Storytimes . . .	. . . Plus
1. Rhymes and Songs	4. Games
There's a Snail in My Bucket	Snail Trail
Snail Crawled Across My Toe	5. Longer Projects
Five Little Snails	Snail Trail Slime
2. Storytime Picks	6. Tell Aloud
Gluey, a Snail Tale by Vivian Walsh	The Turtle and the Snail
Rainy Day Slug by Mary Palenick Colborn	Sammy Snail's Story
Seymour Slug Starts School by Carey Armstrong Ellis	7. Food
The Snail and the Whale by Julia Donaldson	Candy Snail
Snail Boy by Leslie McGuirk	8. Tips
Snail Trail by Ruth Brown	
3. Crafty Corner	
Snail Finger Puppet	

STORYTIMES . . .

Rhymes and Songs

There's a Snail in My Bucket

Tune: There's a Hole in My Bucket

There's a snail in my bucket, he's yucky, he's yucky.
There's a snail in my bucket, oh what should I do?
There's a snail in my bucket, I don't want to touch it.
There's a snail in my bucket, I won't touch it, could you?

There's a snail in my bucket, he's yucky, he's yucky.
There's a snail in my bucket, oh what should I do?
There's a snail in my bucket, Turn it over, turn it over.

There's a snail in my bucket, now he fell on my shoe.

There's no snail in my bucket, he's gone, he's gone.
Now my bucket is empty, and I'll go home too.

Snail Crawled Across My Toe

Tune: Farmer in the Dell

Snail crawled across my toe. *(Point)*
Snail crawled across my toe.
Hi-yo, just watch me go.
Snail crawled across my toe.

Snail crawled across my foot. *(Point)*
Snail crawled across my foot.
Hi-yo, I won't stay put.
Snail crawled across my foot.

Snail crawled across my knee. *(Point)*
Snail crawled across my knee.

Hi-yo, just watch me flee.
Snail crawled across my knee.

Snail crawled across my leg. *(Point)*
Snail crawled across my leg.
Hi-yo, please stop, I'll beg.
Snail crawled across my leg.

Snail crawled across my arm. *(Point)*
Snail crawled across my arm.
Hi-yo, please don't do me harm.
Snail crawled across my arm.

Snail crawled across my head. *(Point)*
Snail crawled across my head.
Hi-yo, I feel some dread.
Snail crawled across my head.

Five Little Snails (*A Counting Rhyme*)

Five little snails, by the backyard door.
One scooted off, and then there were four.

Four little snails crawled around the big oak tree.
One scooted off, and then there were three.

Three little snails, they crawled across my shoe.
One scooted off, and then there were two.

Two little snails, they were having so much fun.
One scooted off, and then there was one.

One little snail, was hot out in the sun.
He scooted off and then there were none.

No little snails out, now they are all gone.
But they left a shiny trail to decorate my lawn.

Storytime Picks

Gluey, a Snail Tale by Vivian Walsh, 2002. A snail and a rabbit learn to live together and help each other out.

Rainy Day Slug by Mary Palenick Colborn, 2000. Written in rhyme, this book follows a little slug around as he goes about on a rainy day.

Seymour Slug Starts School by Carey Armstrong Ellis, 2005. Seymour the slug is nervous about starting slug school until his Fairy Slugmother agrees to help him, but she makes more trouble than help.

The Snail and the Whale by Julia Donaldson, 2004. A snail travels around the world on the tail of a humpback whale and has many adventures.

Snail Boy by Leslie McGuirk, 2003. A giant snail as big as a horse goes looking for an owner.

Snail Trail by Ruth Brown, 2000. This book follows the trail of a snail as he goes about his day. The short text in this book makes it a good choice for younger children.

Crafty Corner

Snail Finger Puppet

Materials: Two colors of felt, stiff metallic elastic string, wiggle eyes, glue, and markers.

Instructions:

1. Cut two identical pieces of the snail from felt *(patterns on page 180)*, using one color for the shell and another for the body.
2. Glue the identical two pieces of the snail body together around all the edges, but leave the bottom unglued. You should be able to open the bottom.
3. Cut two small pieces of the stiff elastic string and slide them in between the two pieces of the head, keeping the ends sticking out. This will be the snail's feelers. Do this while the glue is still soft.

4. Glue the shell pieces onto each side of the snail body, leaving a small area of pink at the bottom.

5. Add wiggle eyes and draw on a smile.

6. Put a small line of glitter or glitter glue on the bottom for a slimy trail.

Alternatives: Use pipe cleaners for the feelers. Use a die cut to cut your snail body. Use the puppet with a popsicle instead of your finger.

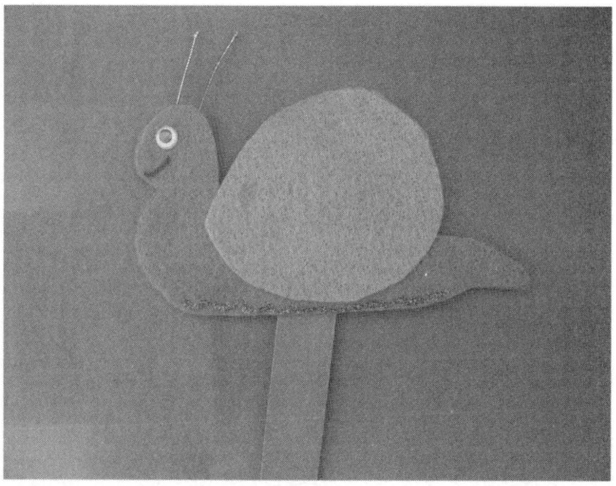

. . . PLUS

Games

Snail Trail

Play this game similar to the game Duck, Duck, Goose. Have the children sit in a circle, and choose one child to walk around the outside of the circle, tapping each child on the head or hand and saying the word "Snail" with each tap.

At any time while walking around the circle, the first child will choose someone sitting in the circle and say the word "Trail" when they tap that child, and then that child will get up and try to catch the first one. They both must stay on the outside of the circle. If the first child makes it all around the circle without getting caught and sits down in the spot where the other was sitting, then the first child may stay there, and the other child starts the game over.

However, the catch is that the children may only run at a "snail's pace," by touching the toe of one foot by the heel of their other foot with each step while moving as quickly as possible. If they don't do this, then the other one instantly wins the spot in the circle.

Longer Projects

Make Snail Trail Slime (also called Goop). Mix together ½ cup corn starch and 1 cup water. You can now tap the mixture with a spoon or your finger and it will be hard. If you slowly put your finger in it, or pour it, it will be liquid. Give each child a small plastic bag or bowl of their own to play with or to take home. Let school-age children mix it themselves.

Tell Aloud

Make flannel board pieces for a flannel story, or tell aloud the story *The Turtle and the Hare*, but change the story so that it is a snail instead of a turtle racing another creature of your choice.

The draw-and-tell *Sammy Snail's Story* can be found on pages 23–24 in the book *More Tell and Draw Stories* by Margaret Jean Oldfield.

Food

Make a candy snail by putting a chocolate-covered cherry on a flat piece of chocolate bar, and put a small marshmallow beside it with a couple of small dots of icing for eyes. Bite into the sticky snail.

Figure 26-1. Snail Finger Puppet

Tips

Use the snail finger puppet, a stuffed animal, or a puppet snail when singing the song *Snail Crawled Across My Toe*, putting the snail on the body part as the song goes.

Bring real snails in a glass aquarium for the children to look at. Let them crawl on dark-colored construction paper to see their trail better.

Program 27

SNEEZES

There are all sorts of sneezes, from big sneezes to little ones. Tell stories of the funny results and chain reactions that occur because of a sneeze and what happens when a sneeze is needed but just won't come out.

Storytimes . . .

1. Rhymes and Songs

The Wind Blew Through the Barn

I've Really Got to Sneeze

The Flea He Sneezed

2. Storytime Picks

Baa-Choo! by Sarah Weeks

Barn Sneeze by Karen B. Winnick

The Big Little Sneeze by Katja Reider

The Big Sneeze by Ruth Brown

The Flea's Sneeze by Lynn Downey

Slop Goes the Soup by Pamela D. Edwards

3. Crafty Corner

Tissue Box

. . . Plus

4. Games

Tissue Toss

5. Longer Projects

Painted Handkerchief

6. Tell Aloud

The Snow Queen with the Cold, Cold Heart

7. Food

Chicken Soup

Cocoa with Marshmallows

8. Tips

STORYTIMES . . .

Rhymes and Songs

The Wind Blew Through the Barn

Tune: The Farmer in the Dell

The wind blew through the barn.
The wind blew through the barn.
The wind blew through; cow went "Moo-choo."
The wind blew through the barn.
Repeat adding the following animals:
Duck went "Quack-choo."
Pig went "Oink-choo."
Horse went "Nigh-choo."
Mouse went "Squeak choo."
Sheep went "Baa-choo."
Hen went "Cluck-choo."

Chick went "Peep-choo."
Rooster went "Cock-a-doodle-choo."
Sue said "Tea might do."

I've Really Got to Sneeze

Tune: She Waded in the Water

Oh my nose is really itching and I've really got to sneeze.
Oh my nose is really itching and I've really got to sneeze.
Oh my nose is really itching and I've really got to sneeze.
But that sneeze won't come out yet, *(clap)* you bet!

Oh I've got my tissue handy and I've really got to sneeze.
Oh I've got my tissue handy and I've really got to sneeze.

107

Oh I've got my tissue handy and I've really
    got to sneeze.
But that sneeze won't come out yet, *(clap)*
    you bet!

Oh I'm covering up my nose because I've re-
    ally got to sneeze.
Oh I'm covering up my nose because I've re-
    ally got to sneeze.
Oh I'm covering up my nose because I've re-
    ally got to sneeze.
But that sneeze won't come out yet, *(clap)*
    you bet!

My nose has stopped its itching; I don't have
    to sneeze no more.
My nose has stopped its itching; I don't have
    to sneeze no more.
My nose has stopped its itching; I don't have
    to sneeze no more.
And now that sneeze has gone away, *(clap)*
    hey!
(Sneeze loudly)

The Flea He Sneezed

Tune: Skip to My Lou

The flea, the flea, the flea he sneezed
The flea, the flea, the flea he sneezed
The flea, the flea, the flea he sneezed
And it woke the rat that morning.

Repeat substituting the following:
The rat, the rat, the rat cried "Shoo!"
And it woke the cat that morning.

The cat, the cat, the cat went "Mew!"
And it woke the bat that morning.

The bat, the bat, the bat he flew.
And it woke the cow that morning.

The cow, the cow, the cow went "Moo!"
And it woke the owl that morning.

The owl, the owl, the owl, went "Whoo!"
And it woke the rooster that morning.

The rooster, the rooster, went "Cock-
    a-doodle-doo."
And it woke the dog that morning.

The dog, the dog, he began to chew.
And it woke the hog that morning.

The hog, the hog, the hog went
    "Eeeeww!"
And it woke the frog that morning.

The frog, the frog, he jumped in a shoe.
And he woke the mouse that morning.

The mouse, the mouse, the mouse, he
    knew.
(Speaking) That the flea needed a tissue.
And they went back to sleep that morning.

Storytime Picks

Baa-Choo! by Sarah Weeks, 2004. Sam the Lamb needs to sneeze, but he cannot get the "choo" out. His friends try to help him finish his sneeze.

Barn Sneeze by Karen B. Winnick, 2002. A wind blows through the barn, causing the cow to sneeze. The cow sneezes, causing a chain reaction that spreads to all the animals.

The Big Little Sneeze by Katja Reider, 2002. When Max sneezes because of the dandelions tickling his nose, all his friends think he is sick, and they try to take care of him, against his protests.

The Big Sneeze by Ruth Brown, 1997. A fly lands on a farmer's nose, causing him to sneeze, which sets off a chain reaction of havoc in the barn.

The Flea's Sneeze by Lynn Downey, 2000. All the animals in the barn are asleep except for the flea, who has to sneeze.

Slop Goes the Soup: A Noisy Warthog Word Book by Pamela D. Edwards, 2001. Warthog sneezes while carrying soup and slop goes the soup. Follow the warthogs as they clean up and prepare the meal again before their friends arrive.

Crafty Corner

Tissue Box

    Materials: A new tissue box, markers or paint, glue, miscellaneous decorations.

Instructions:

1. Color the tissue box with paint or markers. If you use paint, keep the cover on, and tear it off when the paint is dry.
2. Decorate the tissue box using glue, glitter pens, beads, sequins, pom-poms, or whatever you wish.

Alternatives: Instead of paint or markers, cover the tissue box in colored paper, construction paper, pieces of cloth, contact paper, or whatever you choose.

Figure 27-1. Fancy Tissue Box

. . . PLUS

Games

Tissue Toss

Place empty facial tissue boxes at different places on the floor, and toss small beanbags or balls at the boxes attempting to have the items go in the holes. Cut out the entire tops of the boxes if you wish to make the game easier.

Longer Projects

Use fabric paint to decorate a handkerchief, or use a square of light cloth. Make sure you allow plenty of time for the paint to dry before it goes home. Decorate only one side so the other side will remain soft. If you have older children who want to make the handkerchief more detailed, complete one design, let it dry completely, and then paint more detail.

Tell Aloud

Retell the story *The Snow Queen with the Cold, Cold Heart* found in the book *Crazy Gibberish and Other Story Stretches* by Naomi Baltuck, 1993. You can tell the story with only one daughter instead of all three, using the daughter with the cold in her nose who was forever sneezing.

Food

Serve individual serving-size containers of chicken soup or orange juice. If you tell the story *The Snow Queen with the Cold, Cold Heart* serve cocoa with marshmallows. Homeschooled children will enjoy making homemade chicken soup.

Tips

The song *The Flea He Sneezed* was written to go with the book *The Flea's Sneeze* and includes all the creatures in that book. If you don't use the song with the book or if you want to shorten it, then choose only the animals you wish to use or add different ones.

The song *The Wind Blew Through the Barn* was written to go with the book *Barn Sneeze*. Again, you might add or take away any animals when not using the book.

Use a tissue or handkerchief as a prop while singing *I've Really Got to Sneeze*. Talk about good health habits like covering your mouth when you sneeze and washing your hands.

Program 28

SNOW PEOPLE

When the snow starts to fall, it's time to go outside and make snow people. Then you can enjoy stories of magical snow people and their adventures; learn ways to make and decorate your own snowman or how to feed the cold birds in the winter.

Storytimes . . .

1. Rhymes and Songs

Snow Family

I Built Myself a Little Snowman

The Snow Comes Down

See the Snow Falling There

2. Storytime Picks

Bob's Vacation by Dana Meachen Rau

Harry and the Snow King by Ian Whybrow

One Snowy Day by Jeffrey Scherer

Snow Dude by Daniel Kirk

Snowballs by Lois Ehlert

Stella, Queen of the Snow by Marie-Louise Gay

Stranger in the Woods by Carl R. Sams II

3. Crafty Corner

Snowman Ornament

Snow Globe

. . . Plus

4. Games

Pin the Nose on the Snowman

5. Longer Projects

Birdfeeder

Birdhouse

6. Tell Aloud

The Snow Queen with the Cold, Cold Heart

The Rollaway Snowperson

7. Food

Snowballs

Frozen Treats

8. Tips

STORYTIMES . . .

Rhymes and Songs

Snow Family

Tune: It's Raining, It's Pouring

It's snowing. It's snowing.
Our snow family is growing.
I made a dad, I made a mom,
and they're all dressed so pretty.

It's snowing. It's snowing.
Our snow family is growing.
I made a cat and made a dog,
and made two lovely children.

It's snowing. It's snowing.
Our snow family is growing.
Grandma's here, and Grandpa too,
and baby sister dressed in blue.

I Built Myself a Little Snowman

Tune: Mary Had a Little Lamb

I built myself a little snowman,
a little snowman, a little snowman.
I built myself a little snowman
who had a carrot nose.

Repeat with the following lines:
. . . who had two eyes of coal.
. . . who had a button mouth.

… who had a scarf of red.
… who had a hat of blue.
… who had bright buttons of gold
… who had a broom to hold.

The Snow Comes Down (*A Rhyme*)

The snow comes down, *(Wiggle fingers)*
and it builds up high. *(Movie fingers up)*
We'll make a snowball,
just you and I. *(Point)*

Let make the ball bigger, *(Hands form a ball)*
and make it times three. *(Hold up three fingers)*
And it becomes a snowman,
for all to see. *(Point around)*

The snow comes down, *(Repeat)*
and it builds up high. *(Repeat)*

Now let's throw some snowballs,
just you and I. *(Point)*

See the Snow Falling There

Tune: I Love You, You Love Me

See the snow, falling there, *(Point)*
falling, falling everywhere.
We pick up the snow and roll a great big
      ball. *(Roll hands)*
We'll make a snowman round and
      tall.

See the snow, falling there,
falling, falling everywhere.
We'll roll up the snow and throw a tiny ball.
      (Roll and throw)
It will be fun for one and all.

Storytime Picks

Bob's Vacation by Dana Meachen Rau, 2001. Find out from Bob the Snowman what snowmen really do when they go on vacation.

Harry and the Snow King by Ian Whybrow, 1997. Harry builds a snowman, but when it disappears, Harry wants to know where his snowman went.

One Snowy Day by Jeffrey Scherer, 1999. Working together, all the animals make a new winter friend, which is a snowman.

Snow Dude by Daniel Kirk, 2004. A Snow Man comes alive and runs from everyone, in a plot similar to the story of the gingerbread man, but with a happy ending.

Snowballs by Lois Ehlert, 1995. A variety of unusual objects are used to dress snow people and snow pets. The objects used will later feed the hungry birds.

Stella, Queen of the Snow by Marie-Louise Gay, 2005. Stella answers her little brother Sam's every question when he experiences his first snowfall.

Stranger in the Woods by Carl R. Sams II, 2000. Wonderful photographs of real animals in the snow tell a story of finding a snowman in the woods made with things the animals can eat on a cold winder day.

Crafty Corner

Snowman Ornament

Materials: A die-cut snowman shape, elastic string, yarn, assortment of small seeds, kernels, and nuts.

Instructions:

1. Decorate the snowman by gluing on the seeds or nuts for the eyes, mouth, etc.

2. Use markers to draw on a mouth or any other features you don't use seeds for.

3. Tie the yarn around the snowman's neck for a scarf.

4. Glue or tape the elastic string to the back of the snowman so you can hang it up.

Alternatives: Instead of a die cut, draw your own snowman or have the children draw and cut out their own showman shape.

Snow Globe

Materials: Small glass or plastic jars, small plastic or ceramic figures which will fit inside the jars (depicting a winter or holiday other theme), strong glue, glycerin, distilled water, and white glitter.

Instructions:

1. In advance glue the figure on the inside of the jar lid. Allow it to dry completely.

2. Add a few drops of glycerin and a large pinch of white glitter into the jar, and then fill the jar with water to the top and put the lid on tight.

3. Turn the jar over and shake it and you will see the snow falling around the figure.

Alternatives: Use other colors of glitter, and choose a figure to go with other holidays or themes. Paint or decorate the edge of the lid to make it a bit more colorful.

Figure 28-1. Snow Man Ornament

Figure 28-2. Snow Globe

. . . PLUS

Games

Pin the Nose on the Snowman

Make a large snowman, about 4 feet tall, out of poster board or felt (draw three different size circles and cut out), leaving off his nose. Make paper or cardboard carrots (add double-stick tape or Velcro to the back) or use felt. The children can then try to stick the nose to the spot it should go while blindfolded. Let younger preschoolers or toddlers put the nose on without the blindfold.

Longer Projects

Place a birdfeeder platform close to a window or a location that birds come to, and put out a bowl of birdseed. Make a birdfeeder by taking a pine cone, tying a piece of string or yarn around it, and then spreading peanut butter all over the pine cone and then rolling it in birdseed. Keep a log of the types and number of birds you see.

School-age children will enjoy making a simple birdhouse. Find a book on building birdhouses, try an Internet subject search for many birdhouse options, or use a birdhouse kit.

Tell Aloud

Tell the story *The Snow Queen with the Cold Cold Heart* found in *Crazy Gibberish and Other Story Stretches* by Naomi Baltuck on pages 37–41. This story has actions that the children can do and say each time a certain character's name is said. Use props such as a marshmallow with a face drawn on, a small bottle filled with sequins to toss over the audience as a magic potion, rolled-up orange, and yellow crepe paper streamers to toss as lightning bolts.

Make a flannel board story using *The Rollaway Snowperson*, a version of the story of the Gingerbread Man, found on page 33 of *Flannel Graphs* by Jean Stangl.

Food

Serve hot cocoa with marshmallows, popsicles, ice cream, or another frozen treat. Another alternative is to buy the snack cakes called Snowballs or something similar.

Tips

Read the book *Snowballs*, and follow by singing the song *Snow Family*. Put birdseed loose in a decorated box, and let the children guess what is in the box. Give each child a small bag of birdseed to take home and feed the birds.

Make a flannel snowman with no features and add them as you sing the song *I Built Myself a Little Snowman*.

When doing the rhyme *The Snow Comes Down*, hide some small Styrofoam balls and toss them over your audience to imitate snowballs at the end of the rhyme. Have a mock snowball fight.

Program 29

SPAGHETTI DAY

Spaghetti is not only a yummy meal but also a lot of fun, especially as a storytime topic. From runaway food to sharing a meal with friends, this twirly slurpy food will be a big hit.

Storytimes . . .

1. Rhymes and Songs

If You Love Spaghetti

I Like Spaghetti

Another Piece of Spaghetti

2. Storytime Picks

Is the Spaghetti Ready? by Frank B. Edwards

More Spaghetti, I Say! by Rita Golden Gelman

On Top of Spaghetti by Tom Glaser

Spaghetti Eddie by Ryan SanAngelo

Strega Nona by Tomie De Paola

Wednesday Is Spaghetti Day by Maryann Cocca-Leffler

3. Crafty Corner

Spaghetti Head

. . . Plus

4. Games

Spaghetti Jump

Pasta Slurp

5. Longer Projects

Pasta Creations

6. Tell Aloud

Spaghetti Toss and Poem

7. Food

Spaghetti

8. Tips

STORYTIMES . . .

Rhymes and Songs

If You Love Spaghetti

Tune: If You're Happy and You Know It

If you love spaghetti, slurp it up. *(Make slurping sound: "Slurp, slurp")*
If you love spaghetti, slurp it up. *(Slurp, slurp)*
If you love spaghetti and you really like to eat it,
if you love spaghetti, slurp it up. *(Slurp, slurp)*

If you love spaghetti, twirl it around. *(Say "Twirl, twirl" and twirl hand)*
If you love spaghetti, sprinkle it with cheese. *(Say "Shake, shake" and shake hand)*

If you love spaghetti, shout "YUM, YUM!" *(Shout "Yum, Yum!")*
If you love spaghetti, do it all! *(Slurp, slurp; twirl, twirl; shake, shake; "Yum Yum!")*

I Like Spaghetti

Tune: Three Blind Mice

I like spaghetti. I like spaghetti.
It's fun to eat. It's fun to eat.
It is so good and it tastes so nice.
I could eat it all day, and eat it all night.
Did you ever taste such a taste in your life?
As a bowl of spaghetti, a bowl of spaghetti.

I like meatballs. I like meatballs.
They're fun to eat. They're fun to eat.
Sitting there, they are such a great sight.
Piled up on my plate, to such a great height.
Did you ever see such a sight in your life?

As a pile of meatballs, a pile of meatballs.

I like garlic bread. I like garlic bread.
It's fun to eat. It's fun to eat.
It tastes so good but it is so smelly.
I hold my nose and it goes in my belly.
Did you ever smell a smell so smelly?
as a plate of garlic bread, a plate of garlic
    bread.
(Hold your nose)

Another Piece of Spaghetti *(A Rhyme)*

One piece of spaghetti landed on my plate.
I sucked it up *(make sucking noise)* and it
    was just great.

Another piece of spaghetti, that makes two.
I sucked it up *(make sucking noise)* but still
    I'm not through.

Another piece of spaghetti, that makes three.
I sucked it up *(make sucking noise)*, very
    carefully.

Another piece of spaghetti, that makes four.
I sucked it up *(make sucking noise)*, but I
    still want more.

Another piece of spaghetti, that makes five.
I sucked it up *(make sucking noise)*, my fork
    took a dive.

Another piece of spaghetti, that makes six.
I sucked it up *(make sucking noise)*, now my
    fingers I will lick.

Now another piece of spaghetti would make
    my tummy ache.
So I'll quit the spaghetti, and now I'll eat my
    cake.

Storytime Picks

Is the Spaghetti Ready? by Frank B. Edwards, 1998. The zookeeper cooks spaghetti for all the animals, and then they politely wait for her before they start to eat. This is a good book for younger children.

More Spaghetti, I Say! by Rita Golden Gelman, 1999. Freddie the Monkey wants to play with his friend Minnie, but she is too busy eating spaghetti to play. This is also available in a big book.

On Top of Spaghetti by Tom Glaser, 1995. The classic song set in a storybook form, so you can read it or sing it.

Spaghetti Eddie by Ryan Sanangelo, 2002. Eddie loves spaghetti, and he saves the day over and over by using his spaghetti in some very strange ways.

Strega Nona by Tomie De Paola, 1975. This is a Caldecott honor book about an elderly witch and a magic pasta pot. Her gardener Big Anthony secretly tries it out one day with disastrous results.

Wednesday Is Spaghetti Day by Maryann Cocca-Leffler, 1990. Catrina, the cat, and all her friends get together and make spaghetti when her owners leave the house.

Crafty Corner

Spaghetti Head

Materials: A paper plate, stick-on eyes, several different colors of yarn, red reinforcement circles, markers or crayons, and a wooden ruler or paint stick.

Instructions:

1. Precut lots of yarn into small pieces. This will be for the hair, so use a variety of colors and lengths (older children can cut their own yarn). Also, cut a long piece of light-colored yarn to use for the spaghetti piece.

2. In advance, make a hole in the lower part of the plate for the mouth. The children will just need to place a red reinforcement circle over it for lips.

3. Cut the shape of a face *(see Figure 29-1)* on the lower part of the plate.

4. Pull one end of the yarn through the mouth, and knot both ends to prevent it from slipping out.

5. Using the cut yarn, glue all around the top of the paper plate for hair. Be creative with the style, shape, and length.

6. Complete the face by putting on the stick-on eyes and drawing eyelashes, nose, etc.

7. Glue the paper plate onto the ruler, being careful not to cover up the back of the mouth.

Alternatives: Add ribbons or hair clips to make the hair more realistic. To make it easier, don't trim the bottom of the paper plate; just leave it round. Use a large popsicle stick instead of a ruler, or just hold the paper plate head and don't put it on anything.

Figure 29-1. Spaghetti Head

...PLUS

Games

Spaghetti Jump

Bring in several jump ropes in a large basket or bowl (to resemble spaghetti). Have jump rope contests to see who can go longer, higher, and so forth.

Pasta Slurp

Have a pasta-eating contest. This will be a good game for homeschoolers during a spaghetti dinner. See who can make the most noise while sucking in a long piece of cooked spaghetti, or see who can eat it the fastest, and so on. Use plain spaghetti or spaghetti with sauce. Wear aprons and old clothes to avoid mess.

Longer Projects

Make pasta creations by gluing colored pasta to picture frames, boxes, or other objects, or make necklaces. As a project, let the children color the pasta. Cover dry pasta with rubbing alcohol and add food coloring until it is the desired color. Then dry the pasta completely on wax paper. Be sure to use rubber gloves to prevent the food coloring from staining your hands.

Make gift boxes or frames by changing the color of your pasta to suit the occasion, for example, red for Valentine's Day or green and red for Christmas.

Tell Aloud

Read the poem *Spaghetti*, found in the book **A Light in the Attic** by Shel Silverstein. While you are saying the poem, hold a large bowl filled with cut-up yarn, but don't show the children what is in the bowl. At the end of the poem, suddenly start tossing the yarn over the children; they will think you are tossing real spaghetti on them. For younger children who might not follow a longer poem, use the following poem.

I Just Love Spaghetti *(A Poem)*

I just love spaghetti.
I just love it I do.
I just love spaghetti.
Would you like some too?

You say you want spaghetti
and that you love it too.
Well here's the spaghetti,
it's falling on YOU! *(Toss yarn)*

Food

Homeschoolers can plan and prepare a spaghetti dinner. Use small individual cans of spaghetti or pasta; hand out something simple such as garlic-flavored crackers, or use candy in long, thin strips, such as licorice strips or soda straw candy.

Tips

Make flannel pieces to go with the song *I Like Spaghetti*, and put the pieces up on a flannel board as you sing the song.

Older children will enjoy the book *The Ravioli Kid* by Michelle Freedman. The evil Angel Hair and his gang of anti-pasta come to the town of El Pasta to steal the golden ravioli, until the Ravioli Kid saves the day.

While saying the rhyme *Another Piece of Spaghetti*, have the children all make the sucking noise along with you. Make the Spaghetti Head craft and have everyone use it during the rhyme to pull the spaghetti through the mouth and make the sucking sound.

Program 30

TALE OF TAILS

There are short tails, long tails, furry tails, and more, and there are lots of tales to go with them. From legends to silly new combinations or just normal tails and how they wag, you'll have no trouble picking a tail to tell about.

Storytimes . . .

1. Rhymes and Songs

If I Had a Tail

All the Little Doggies

The Tail Song

2. Storytime Picks

If I Had a Tail by Karen Clemens Warrick

The Perfect Tail by Mie Araki

The Silly Tale Book by Marc Brown

Tales of Tails by Gene-Michael Higney

Tom's Tale by Arlene Dubanevich

Where's My Tail? by Susan Schafer

Why Epossumondas Has No Hair on His Tail by Coleen Salley

3. Crafty Corner

Animal Tails

. . . Plus

4. Games

Pin the Tail on What?

5. Longer Projects

Tail Center

6. Tell Aloud

Why Mr. Bear Has a Short Tail

All the Little Doggies

7. Food

Animal Crackers

8. Tips

STORYTIMES . . .

Rhymes and Songs

If I Had a Tail

Tune: London Bridge

If only I had a tail, had a tail, had a tail.
If only I had a tail, what would I be?

If my tail was long and furry,
Long and furry, long and furry,
if my tail was long and furry, what would I be?

If my tail went wag, wag, wag;
wag, wag, wag; wag, wag, wag,
if my tail went wag, wag, wag, what would I be?

If my tail was curly and short,
curly and short, curly and short,
if my tail was curly and short, what would I be?

If my tail was scaly and green,
scaly and green, scaly and green,
if my tail was scaly and green, what would I be?

If my tail was short and fluffy,
short and fluffy, short and fluffy,
if my tail was short and fluffy, what would I be?

If my tail was long and thin,
long and thin, long and thin,
if my tail was long and thin, what would I be?

If my tail helped me jump,

helped me jump, helped me jump,
if my tail helped me jump, what would I be?

If my tail had many colors,
many colors, many colors,
if my tail had many colors, what would I be?

All the Little Doggies *(A Rhyme)*

Five little doggies out in the snow, *(Hold up five fingers)*
Five little tails wagged to and fro. *(Wag finger)*
Soon the front door opened wide, *(Spread hands)*
And a little boy said, "Come on inside!" *(Gesture)*
And the doggie went, "Bark!" Then the doggie went in.
(Repeat verse, counting down 4, 3, 2, 1, increasing barks)

Four little doggies out in the snow, *(Hold up four fingers)* . . .
And the doggie went, "Bark! Bark!" Then the doggie went in.

No little doggies out in the snow,
No little tails wagging to and fro. *(Wag finger)*
The little boy let them in and when they had been well fed
All the little doggies were asleep inside their bed.

The Tail Song

Tune: I Love You, You Love Me

I'll wag here, I'll wag there.
I will wag, wag, anywhere.
I'm a tail on a dog, begging for a bone.
I have one now, so I'll go home.

Storytime Picks

If I Had a Tail by Karen Clemens Warrick, 2001. A story told in rhyme which lets you guess to whom each tail belongs.

The Perfect Tail by Mie Araki, 2004. Fred likes the tails on all the other animals but finally finds that his own tail works best for him.

The Silly Tale Book by Marc Brown, 1994. This is a silly story, by the creator of the Arthur series, about the many different kinds of tails that animals have, plus some silly pictures of "what if" combinations.

Tales of Tails by Gene-Michael Higney, 2000. A lift-the-flap book with rhyming text shows what different tails do.

Tom's Tale by Arlene Dubanevich, 1990. Old Tom is sleeping too much and the mice are taking over, until Tom gives them a surprise.

Where's My Tail? by Susan Schafer, 2005. A little lizard loses his tail after having a close call when chased by a bobcat. He doesn't know that lizards' tails grow back, so he sets out to look for his tail.

Why Epossumondas Has No Hair on His Tail by Coleen Salley, 2004. A young possum who has a human mama asks her why he has no hair on his tail, and she tells him the legend behind it.

Crafty Corner

Animal Tails

Materials: Die cuts of several different animals and materials to use for their tails (pom-poms, feathers, string, pipe cleaners, etc.).

Instructions:

1. Glue different objects on the die-cut animals to represent their tails. Examples: a curling pipe cleaner on a pig; feathers on a bird or peacock; pom-poms on rabbits, lions, dogs, or bears.

2. Glue on wiggle eyes and draw mouths and whiskers where needed.

Alternatives: Use magnets for a refrigerator decoration, or glue on popsicle sticks to use them as stick puppets, or mount them on paper and draw a background for a picture. Create brand new animals with unusual tails.

Figure 30-1. Animal Tails

. . . PLUS

Games

Pin the Tail on What?

Play like Pin the Tail on the Donkey, but use a different animal besides the donkey. Draw a large picture of an animal on poster board, flannel, or butcher paper. Choose an animal with a distinctive tail. Put Velcro on a large pom-pom for a rabbit, double-stick tape on large feathers for a bird, a long piece of felt with the ends fringed for a lion or Eeyore tail, and so on.

Longer Projects

Create a tail center by putting out a variety of pictures and books about different animals with tails. Add writing and drawing materials so the children can write a story about their animal, draw pictures, or perhaps make up and draw a new animal by combining one animal's tail on a different animal's body.

Tell Aloud

Make a flannel from the legend *Why Mr. Bear Has a Short Tail*. This story is available in different versions of story books, and a good flannel board version can be found in the book *Teeny-Tiny Folktales* compiled by Jean Warren.

Make flannel dogs with a variety of tails, and hand them out to the children. Say the rhyme *All the Little Doggies*, and ask the children who have a dog with a short tail to bring up their dog to the flannel board. Repeat the rhyme with a long thin tail, a long fluffy tail, a long tail with a big puff at the end, a shaggy tail, and so on.

Food

Serve animals crackers and milk. Shake cookies in a bowl for each child, and let them see how many different kinds of tails are in each of their bowls.

Tips

School-age children will enjoy *The Spooky Tale of Prewitt Peacock* by Bill Peet. This is a long story about a little peacock whose tail is different from all the other peacocks, so they try to drive him away, but in the end his tail saves them all. This story shows how it is ok to be different. Afterward, have the children design their own picture of a peacock with an unusual tail. They can design the tail using feathers, markers, and other materials.

When singing the song *If I Had a Tail*, use a variety of puppets or stuffed animals that represent different tails in the song. Keep them hidden from view in a sack or box. After each verse, ask the children to guess what the animal is, and then pull out the puppet.

There are several different Winnie-the-Pooh books about Eeyore losing his tail. Read your favorite. Make an Eeyore tail (or one for each child) and hide it so the children can search and find it.

Sing the traditional song of **Where, Oh Where Has My Little Dog Gone**, and after singing the part "With his tail cut short," repeat and substitute other types of tails.

Program 31

THANKFUL FOR

There are many things that we are all thankful for, from your loved ones to that scrumptious pie at the end of your Thanksgiving dinner. Explore stories about the many things that are enjoyed, laughed at, and appreciated by all.

Storytimes . . .

1. Rhymes and Songs

I'm Thankful For

One Little Child on Thanksgiving Day

Turkey! Turkey!

I'm Thankful, I'm Thankful

2. Storytime Picks

Biscuit Is Thankful by Alyssa Satin Capucilli

I Know an Old Lady Who Swallowed a Pie by Alison Jackson

The Most Thankful Thing by Lisa McCourt

Thank You, Thanksgiving by David Milgrim

Thanks for Thanksgiving by Julie Markes

Thanksgiving at the Tappletons' by Eileen Spinelli

Thanksgiving Cats by Jean Marzollo

3. Crafty Corner

Thankful Card

. . . Plus

4. Games

Thanksgiving Pie

5. Longer Projects

Thankful Book

Food Collection

6. Tell Aloud

I Know an Old Lady Who Swallowed a Pie

I'm Thankful Poem

Running Bear's Thanksgiving

7. Food

Thanksgiving Treats

8. Tips

STORYTIMES . . .

Rhymes and Songs

I'm Thankful For

Tune: The Bear Went Over the Mountain

I'm thankful for my family.
I'm thankful for my family.
I'm thankful for my family,
On this Thanksgiving Day.

Repeat with:
I'm thankful for my friends.
I'm thankful for the food we have.
I'm thankful that I can run and
    play.

One Little Child on Thanksgiving Day (*A Flannel Rhyme*)

One little child on Thanksgiving Day,
sat with the others, and he did say:
I'm thankful for so many things,
but I'm not thankful for the peas.

Repeat with:
. . . for the broccoli
. . . for the radishes
. . . for the beans
. . . for the carrots
(*Substitute any other vegetables you wish*)
Last verse:
All the little children on Thanksgiving
    Day
sat all together and they did say,

We're thankful for so many things.
now the turkey's here, let's eat!

Turkey! Turkey!

Tune: Skip to My Lou

Turkey, turkey, wobble to your left *(Go left, flap arms)*
Turkey, turkey, wobble to your right *(Go right)*
Turkey, turkey, better get out of sight. *(Kneel down)*
Farmer's coming in the morning. *(Get up, point)*

Turkey, turkey, wobble all around *(Go in a circle, flap arms)*
Turkey, turkey, jump up and down *(Hop twice)*
Turkey, turkey, don't make a sound. *(Finger over lips)*

Farmer's coming in the morning. *(Point)*

Turkey, turkey ran so fast *(Run in circle, flap arms)*
Turkey, turkey safe at last *(Hop twice)*
Turkey, turkey hiding in the barn. *(Flap wings)*
Farmer's gonna eat peas and corn.

I'm Thankful, I'm Thankful

Tune: It's Raining, It's Pouring

I'm thankful, I'm thankful
I am so very thankful
for mom and dad and sister too
I am so very thankful.

Repeat with:
for grandma and my grandpa too
for my brother and all my friends
for doggy, kitty, and my fish
for this meal and chocolate pie

Storytime Picks

Biscuit Is Thankful by *Alyssa Satin Capucilli*, 2003. Every day Biscuit the Puppy finds things he is thankful for, and his owner is thankful for Biscuit.

I Know an Old Lady Who Swallowed a Pie by Alison Jackson, 1997. Based on the classic rhyme **I Know an Old Lady Who Swallowed a Fly**, this old lady swallows a Thanksgiving pie, and lots of other things with it.

The Most Thankful Thing by Lisa McCourt, 2004. A little girl tries to guess what her mama is the most thankful for by looking through her photograph album.

Thank You, Thanksgiving by David Milgrim, 2003. A little girl goes through Thanksgiving Day thinking of all the many things that she is thankful for.

Thanks for Thanksgiving by Julie Markes, 2004. In this book with big colorful illustrations, children name all the things they are thankful for.

Thanksgiving at the Tappletons' by Eileen Spinelli, 2004. This newly illustrated edition shows a family of wolves who learn to celebrate Thanksgiving through family and not food.

Thanksgiving Cats by Jean Marzollo, 1999. In this story, told in rhyme, a family of farmer cats grow vegetables, cook together, and have Thanksgiving dinner.

Crafty Corner

Thankful Card

Materials: Orange or brown construction paper, material for decorations (die-cut leaves or flowers, plastic leaves, glitter, pictures cut from magazines, stickers, etc.), markers or crayons, and glue.

Instructions:

1. Fold your construction paper in half, and then open it like a greeting card.

2. In advance, print the words "Thankful for You" (or whatever you choose for you card to say) on white or light paper. Cut around the words and glue the message

inside the card, or print the words from your computer, cut them out, and glue them inside.

3. Decorate the card, both the front and inside, using the die cuts, plastic leaves, glitter, pictures cut from magazines, stickers, and so on.

Alternatives: Use paint, photographs, or pictures cut from Thanksgiving invitations or napkins, or other materials. Write your message on paper with a marker instead of on the computer.

Figure 31-1. Thankful Card

...PLUS

Games

Thanksgiving Pie
Cut pie shapes out of sponges. Have two children face each other holding pie pans, and toss the sponge pies to each other and attempt to catch the pie in the pan. An alternative would be to throw the shapes toward a group and see who can catch the most pies.

Longer Projects

Make a Thankful Book. Use the instructions for the craft in the theme *Read to Me (see pages 96–97)* to make the book. Children can make their book by writing, drawing pictures with crayons or markers, or using die cuts or magazine pictures in order to list different things they are thankful for. Decorate the book similar to your Thankful For card in fall colors.

Collect canned and dried food for the needy. Prepare a basket or box for the children to put things in that they bring.

Tell Aloud

Instead of reading the book *I Know an Old Lady Who Swallowed a Pie*, you can use it to make a very cute flannel story. Make multiple old ladies to have her grow fatter and fatter as she eats. To save a little time, make one head and switch out the different-size bodies as she grows. Point to the different items as you say the verses, which will make it easier for the children to repeat them along with you.

The flannel *I'm Thankful Poem* can be found in *The Best of Totline Flannelboards* by Totline on page 68.

The tell-aloud story *Running Bear's Thanksgiving* can be found on page 19 of *Short-Short Stories* compiled by Jean Warren. It's the story of Running Bear, a young Native American, who has been invited to a celebration with his friends the pilgrims. He worries because he has nothing to take until a surprise event happens.

Figure 31-2. Old Lady Who Swallowed a Pie (Flannel Board Example)

Food

Serve Thanksgiving treats such as small pecan tarts or cookies. Bake a pecan or pumpkin pie from scratch. Bake cornbread muffins. Serve apple cider or apple juice.

Tips

When singing the song *I'm Thankful For*, use props such as people puppets to represent the ones in the song and a piece of fake food. For the last line, hop around or use the people puppets again.

Say the rhyme *One Little Child on Thanksgiving Day* and follow by having the children tell foods that they don't like to eat and what is their favorite Thanksgiving food.

Make flannel pieces of different kinds of vegetables *(patterns on pages 181–183)* to use with the rhyme *One Little Child on Thanksgiving Day*, and point out the vegetables in the verses as you sing.

Program 32

TOOTH FAIRY'S COMING

Everyone wonders about the tooth fairy, what she's like, and how she got started. Here is your chance to explore the stories and legends about this mysterious creature and learn about all the different kinds of teeth that exist, both human and animal.

Storytimes . . .

1. Rhymes and Songs

Where's My Tooth?

I Have a Loose Tooth

I'm a Toothbrush

2. Storytime Picks

Clarabella's Teeth by An Vrombaut

Mabel the Tooth Fairy and How She Got Her Job by Katie Davis

Nice Try, Tooth Fairy by Mary W. Olson

The Night Before the Tooth Fairy by Natasha Wing

The Seed Bunny by Jennifer Selby

The Tooth Book by Theo LeSieg

3. Crafty Corner

Tooth Fairy Tooth Holder

Tooth Fairy Wand

. . . Plus

4. Games

Cavities

5. Longer Projects

Tooth Chart

Field Trip

Tooth Art Center

6. Tell Aloud

Hank and the Tooth Fairy

7. Food

Carrot and Dip

Candy Teeth

8. Tips

STORYTIMES . . .

Rhymes and Songs

Where's My Tooth? *(An Action Rhyme)*

My tooth is loose, see it wiggle,
   Uh-oh!
My tooth is gone, *(Look around)*
now where did it go?

It could be here. *(Point)* It could be there.
   (Point)
It could be just about anywhere.
Who can find my tooth? *(Put up flannel tooth)*
Is this my tooth? *(Ask audience)*
"No!"

(Repeat verse, but use different flannel teeth. For the last tooth, use one that looks like a human tooth.)
"Yes!"

Last verse:
Well my tooth is back, and I won't tarry.
It'll go under my pillow, for the tooth fairy.

I Have a Loose Tooth

Tune: Frere Jacques

I have a loose tooth. I have a loose tooth.
See it move. See it move.
(Pretend to wiggle tooth)

Wiggle, wiggle, wiggle; wiggle, wiggle,
    wiggle,
'til it's out, 'til it's out.

I have a loose tooth. I have a loose tooth.
It's in my hand. It's in my hand.
(Hold out hand and point)
Wiggle, wiggle, wiggle; wiggle, wiggle, wig-
    gle,
Now it's out. Now it's out.

I have a loose tooth. I have a loose tooth.
What do I do? What do I do? *(Shrug)*
Put it under my pillow, put it under my pil-
    low,
and go to sleep, and go to sleep. *(Hand on
    hand)*

I have a loose tooth. I have a loose tooth.
Now it's gone. Now it's gone. *(Hold up
    empty hand)*
Wiggle, wiggle, wiggle; wiggle, wiggle, wig-
    gle,

Tooth fairy came. Tooth fairy came. *(Hold
    up quarter in hand)*

I'm a Toothbrush *(An Action Rhyme)*

I'm a toothbrush. Just watch me go.
I am brushing to and fro. *(Jump side to side)*

I'm a toothbrush. The best you've ever
    found.
I am brushing around and around. *(Turn
    around)*

I'm a toothbrush. I'll keep away the plaque.
I am brushing in the front, then the back.
    (Jump forward and backward)

I'm a toothbrush. Now don't you frown.
I am brushing up and down. *(Jump up and
    down)*

I'm a toothbrush. If you brush awhile
I will give you a pretty smile. *(Smile, point
    to mouth)*

Storytime Picks

Clarabella's Teeth by An Vrombaut, 2003. A crocodile spends so much time brushing her teeth that she doesn't have enough time to play.

Mabel the Tooth Fairy and How She Got Her Job by Katie Davis, 2003. The story of how the tooth fairy was led to collect teeth from children because of her own poor dental habits.

Nice Try, Tooth Fairy by Mary W. Olson, 2000. Emma wants the tooth fairy to bring back her tooth so she can show her grandfather, but the tooth fairy keeps getting the teeth mixed up.

The Night Before the Tooth Fairy by Natasha Wing, 2003. The tale of a little boy with a stubborn tooth.

The Seed Bunny by Jennifer Selby, 1997. A bunny receives a visit from the tooth bunny, and gets carrot seeds instead of money.

The Tooth Book by Theo LeSieg, 1981. A simple story told in rhyme, about all kinds of teeth.

Crafty Corner

Tooth Fairy Tooth Holder (Created by Kathy Lane)

Materials: Different colors of flannel, yarn, die cuts, small hole punch, and glue.

Instructions:

1. Cut a flannel piece using a girl or boy die cut and a small butterfly die cut.
2. Cut a rectangle shape out of another piece of flannel.
3. Glue the butterfly to the back of the flannel child to look like wings.
4. Glue the flannel child to the rectangle shape leaving the top and inside of the butter-fly shape unglued and open so a tooth can be slipped inside.

5. If you wish to hang the pillow up, make small holes in the top of the rectangle and insert a piece of yarn through, to hang the tooth holder. Otherwise slip it under the pillow to help keep the tooth from getting lost.

Alternatives: Trim the edges of the flannel piece with scalloped-type scissors. If you don't have the correct dies, substitute another figure to glue on your square pillow shape (such as a tooth shape or heart shape). For a real pillow, make two of the flannel pieces, glue or sew together, leaving an opening, turn the seams inside, stuff it with batting, and close the opening.

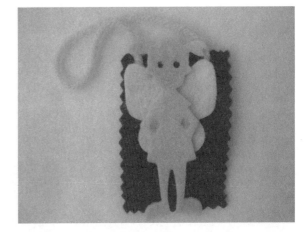

Figure 32-1. Tooth Fairy Tooth Holder

Tooth Fairy Wand

Materials: Card stock or metallic paper, a popsicle stick, and ribbon.

Instructions:

1. Cut a star shape out of a metallic-looking thick paper. If the paper is plain, cover it in shiny paper, glitter, foil, crayons, etc.
2. Paint the popsicle stick or cover it with foil.
3. Glue or tape the star to the stick and glue or tape on ribbons to the star.

Alternatives: Use a straw or piece of rounded wood for the end of the wand. Use a glitter pen or glue and glitter to outline the star.

Figure 32-2. Tooth Fairy Wand

. . . PLUS

Games

Cavities

Make a very large drawing of the outline of a tooth and put it on the wall. Hand out sticky hands or putty and let the children throw it at the tooth so it will stick on and be the cavities. If you laminate it so the sticky mess won't soak in, the children can wipe it off using toothbrushes.

Longer Projects

Make a chart, a graph, or a poster to record when the children lose a tooth. Take a picture of the child showing the empty space, and take another picture after the new tooth grows in. See who loses the most teeth by the end of the year.

Take a field trip to a dentist's office, or invite one to speak to the class or during a storytime. Order or ask a toothbrush company or dentist to donate plaque-disclosing tablets to send home with the children. After you brush your teeth, the tablets coat your gums red to show you how much you missed when you brushed.

Have a tooth art center. Dip dental floss in paint and swirl around to make a picture, or use a toothbrush to paint a picture.

Tell Aloud

Hank and the Tooth Fairy is a draw-and-tell story of a cowboy who gets a wish from the tooth fairy and is on pages 72–78 in *Frog's Riddle and Other Draw-and-Tell Stories* by Richard Thompson.

Food

Read *The Seed Bunny* and pass out small carrots and dip or sunflower seeds. You can find candy teeth by doing a subject search under "candy teeth." Hand out small candies coated in white such as yogurt-covered nuts or raisins to resemble teeth.

Tips

Read *The Seed Bunny*, and send each child home with a small plastic bag filled with carrot seeds. Photocopy and trim the picture of the seed packet in the back of the book and put it in the bag.

Make a variety of flannel teeth *(see patterns on page 179)* to use when reciting the rhyme *Where's My Tooth*. Pass out the flannel teeth to the children, and let them bring up their flannel teeth to the flannel board. You can also use the teeth while reading the story *Nice Try, Tooth Fairy*.

Program 33

TRAIN TRIP

Trains are fascinating, whether they are real ones, toys, or fantasy trains that travel only in your own imagination. Get on board and make your storytime a grand adventure with these mighty machines.

Storytimes . . .

1. Rhymes and Songs

Little Train Engine
Waiting by the Train
Freight Train

2. Storytime Picks

Chugga Chugga Choo Choo by Kevin Lewis
I Love Trains! by Philemon Sturges
Inside Freight Train by Donald Crews
Niccolini's Song by Chuck Wilcoxen
Runaway Train illustrated by Jess Stockham
Train Song by Harriet Ziefert
Two Little Trains by Margaret Wise Brown

3. Crafty Corner

Freight Train Picture

. . . Plus

4. Games

Train Cars

5. Longer Projects

Model Train
Field Trip

6. Tell Aloud

The Little Engine That Could

7. Food

Candy Train

8. Tips

STORYTIMES . . .

Rhymes and Songs

Little Train Engine *(A Rhyme)*

Choo-choo, choo-coo, as it goes,
this little train just grows and grows.
(Repeat this before each verse)

Choo-choo, choo-choo, little car of red.
"All-aboard," the engineer said.

Choo-choo, choo-choo, little car of green.
Cutest little train car you have ever seen.

Choo-choo, choo-choo, what a jolly fellow.
This little train car is painted yellow.

Choo-choo, choo-choo, what do we do?
Let's go ride in the little car of blue.

Choo-choo, choo-choo, little car of black.
Jump on the train and don't look back.

Choo-choo, choo-choo, see the car of pink,
As we pass the station, let's all give a wink.

Choo-choo, choo-choo, orange car is coming.
We're picking up speed, the engine is humming.

Choo-choo, choo-choo, little car of gray.
Do you want to ride on the train today?

Choo-choo, choo-choo, little car of brown.
We ride in the country and we ride in town.

Choo-choo, choo-choo, little car of white.
We've been riding all day and now it's night.

Choo-choo, choo-choo, the train is here.
We're back at the station, let's all give a
cheer. *(Shout "Hooray!")*

Waiting by the Train

Tune: Down by the Station

Standing with their suitcase,
so early in the morning,
five little children,
were waiting by the train.
They're going on vacation,
off on an adventure,
the train pulls up
Toot! Toot! *(Imitate pulling whistle)*
One gets on.
Repeat counting down: four, three, two, one.

Last verse:
Now there are no more little children,
early in the morning,
standing with their suitcase,
waiting for the train.
They've all set off to visit,
all kinds of different places.
When will we see them next?
When they get home.

Freight Train

Tune: Ten Little Indians

Oh engine, stock car, and gondola,
Hopper, tender, tank, and ice car,
Box car, flat car, and caboose,
Freight train's on its way.

Oh engine, stock car, and gondola,
Hopper, tender, tank, and ice car,
Box car, flat car, and caboose;
Freight train's home for the day.

Storytime Picks

Chugga Chugga Choo Choo by Kevin Lewis, 1999. In a rhyming text, a toy train comes to life.

I Love Trains! by Philemon Sturges, 2001. A little boy describes in rhyme the train cars that pass by.

Inside Freight Train by Donald Crews, 2001. A sliding door shows what's inside all the different cars of the freight train.

Niccolini's Song by Chuck Wilcoxen, 2004. A train conductor sings the trains to sleep at night. Soon parents start to bring their babies to hear Niccolini sing. One windy night there are so many people that come, no one can hear Niccolini sing, so the trains sing for him.

Runaway Train illustrated by Jess Stockham, 2004. A train on a ribbon travels through many places around the world.

Train Song by Harriet Ziefert, 2000. A rhyming verse describes each train car that goes by.

Two Little Trains by Margaret Wise Brown, 2001. The parallel journey of two trains. One is real; the other is a toy.

Crafty Corner

Freight Train Picture

Materials: Sheet of long construction or manila paper, quilt batting, die-cut train cars, markers.

Instructions:

1. Glue the train cars onto the paper, connecting the cars.
2. Draw on a train track with markers or glue on pieces of paper, and add whatever background you desire (mountains, meadows, etc.).
3. Pull apart the batting, glue it on as smoke; arrange it so it appears to be coming out of the smokestack of the engine.

Alternatives: Use longer paper, such as 11×17, to add more train cars. Buy precut train shapes. Put people or animal stickers in the windows of the train. Make a frame for your picture by adding strips of construction paper or craft foam.

Figure 33-1. Freight Train Picture

. . . PLUS

Games

Train Cars
A follow-the-leader game where one child is the engine and the others are the train cars. All the children stand behind the engine and hold a shoulder with one hand and use their other hand to make train wheel motions while saying "Choo-choo" together. The child who is the engine leads the rest as they move about the room.

Longer Projects

Bring in a toy or model train and set it up on a table. Older children participate in building a little town for their train by decorating the table, bringing small toy people and animals from home and making houses and fields using construction paper, papier mâché, paint, and other materials. Have an ongoing project to add to the train scene.

Plan a field trip to a train yard or train museum. Write stories about the trip.

Instead of making the craft an individual picture, have each child make a train car and put them on the wall, connecting the individual cars to make a long train that everyone contributed to.

Tell Aloud

Tell the story aloud of the classic tale ***The Little Engine That Could***. The children can repeat "I Think I Can" with you. Afterward, ask children to tell about something they didn't think they could do but were finally able to do.

Food

Prepare a candy train by gluing a package of Lifesavers candy to a packet of gum for the base. Add a Hershey's Kiss candy on top of the lifesavers on one end for the smokestack and a caramel at the other for the engine room. Glue on four peppermints for the wheels.

Tips

Older children will enjoy the book ***Jingle the Brass*** by Patricia Newman, 2004. An engineer takes a boy on a train ride. It is filled with the special words that railroad workers use.

While saying the rhyme ***Little Train Engine***, make flannel train cars in all the different colors from rhyme. Put them on the flannel board as you say the rhyme, or pass them out to the children and let them bring up the cars to the flannel board. Have different shades of some of the colors (such as light blue, dark blue, navy blue, and aqua) so the children can learn that some colors have many shades and variations.

Invite a model train builder to visit your class or storytime and bring some model trains to see.

As you sing the song *Waiting by the Train*, encourage all the children to help make the "Toot, toot!" sound, and imitate pulling the whistle rope.

Program 34

TURKEY TROT

Turkeys are the main event at Thanksgiving, and there are many adventures to share about these funny birds. Tell about turkeys on the run or turkeys sitting down to that special Thanksgiving dinner themselves. You can choose their adventure.

Storytimes . . .

1. Rhymes and Songs

Turkey Hunting We Will Go

Run Little Turkey

Five Little Turkeys

2. Storytime Picks

Five Little Turkeys by William Boniface

Setting the Turkeys Free by W. Nikola-Lisa

Ten Fat Turkeys by Tony Johnston

This Is the Turkey by Abby Levine

A Turkey for Thanksgiving, by Eve Bunting

'Twas the Night Before Thanksgiving by Dav Pilkey

3. Crafty Corner

Turkey Refrigerator Magnet

. . . Plus

4. Games

Turkey Hunt

5. Longer Projects

Painting

6. Tell Aloud

Turkey Feathers

The Turkey Tale

7. Food

Turkey Cookie

8. Tips

STORYTIMES . . .

Rhymes and Songs

Turkey Hunting We Will Go

Tune: A Hunting We Will Go

Turkey hunting we will go. *(March)*
Turkey hunting we will go.
Look for turkey, high and low. *(Look high, then low)*
Turkey hunting we will go. *(March)*

The moose looks all around. *(Look around)*
The moose looks all around.
Look for turkey, high and low. *(Repeat)*
The moose looks all around.

The rabbit joins the moose. *(Jump)*
The rabbit joins the moose.

Look for turkey, high and low.
The rabbit joins the moose.

Repeat substituting verses with:
The goats join the rabbit . . .
The sheep joins the goats . . .
The porcupine joins the sheep . . .

They all catch a turkey. They all catch a turkey.
Looking for turkey, high and low,
They all catch a turkey.

The turkey is their guest. The turkey is their guest.
The guest of honor, Thanksgiving Day,
The turkey is their guest.

Run Little Turkey

Tune: Little Bunny Foo-Foo

One little turkey running through the barn-
yard.
(Hold up one finger, and bop up and down)
Farmer's looking everywhere, far and wide.
(Look all around)
Here comes Mr. Farmer, don't you let him
see you.
*(Use finger of other hand, and bop up and
down)*
Stomp, Stomp, *(Stomp each foot)*
Flap, flap, run and hide. *(Flap your arms)*
(Repeat with two, three, four, five)
Two little turkeys running through the barn-
yard.
Farmer's looking everywhere, far and wide.
Here comes Mr. Farmer, don't you let him
see you. Stomp, stomp, flap, flap, run
and hide.
(Count as high as you wish)

Five Little Turkeys *(A Rhyme)*

Five little turkeys sat in a pen.
"Hide, turkeys, hide! said the little red hen.*
One turkey ran out through the barn door.
And when he was gone, there were only
four.

*(Repeat using first two verses and counting
down)*
One turkey hid where the farmer could not
see.
And when he was gone, there were only
three.

One little turkey ran and jumped and flew.
And when he was gone, there were only
two.

One turkey ran when he saw the farmer's
gun.
And when he was gone, there was only
one.

That turkey jumped down and he begin to
run.
And when he was gone, then there were
none.

Now no little turkeys were sitting in the
pen.
They have all been warned by the little red
hen.
When the farmer came by, with his chef's
hat on.
He found himself in that pen all alone.

Storytime Picks

Five Little Turkeys by William Boniface, 2003. A board book that counts down the turkeys and has a pop-up page at the end.

Setting the Turkeys Free by W. Nikola-Lisa, 2004. A boy paints turkeys and they take on a life of their own. He builds them a turkey pen and then must rescue them from a fox.

Ten Fat Turkeys by Tony Johnston, 2004. A count-down book in which the ten silly turkeys sitting on the fence leave in very creative ways.

This Is the Turkey by Abby Levine, 2000. In the rhyme pattern of "This Is the House That Jack Built," a family celebrates Thanksgiving Day, even after a disaster happens to the turkey.

A Turkey for Thanksgiving by Eve Bunting, 1991. Mr. and Mrs. Moose want a turkey for Thanksgiving, but as a guest, not as the dinner.

'Twas the Night Before Thanksgiving by Dav Pilkey, 1990. Set to the rhyme of " 'Twas the Night Before Christmas," the children take a field trip to a turkey farm and decide to rescue the turkeys.

Crafty Corner

Turkey Refrigerator Magnet

Materials: Flat ice cream spoons, wiggle eyes, red and yellow craft foam, several colors of paint, and magnet pieces.

---

*The first two lines are from Ten Little Turkeys, original author unknown. The rest is completely revised.

Instructions:

1. Prepare the spoons in advance by painting five spoons per person, each a different color, including one brown spoon for the turkey body. Or you can make all the feathers the same color.

2. Using the craft foam, cut a waddle out of the red and a beak from the yellow. Glue this to the brown spoon, on the larger rounded part to be the head. Add the wiggle eyes.

3. Glue the other spoons to the back of the brown, with the small part to the bottom. Spread the tops out so they all show; these are the turkey feathers.

4. Add the magnet to the back so it will stick on a refrigerator.

Figure 34-1. Turkey Refrigerator Magnet

Alternatives: For a quicker and easier way, spray paint (adults only) the spoons, or buy them already painted. Glue them on the top of a napkin ring *(see page 45)*. Use craft foam pieces shaped like feathers.

...PLUS

Games

Turkey Hunt

This is played similar to Marco-Polo. Blindfold someone for the farmer, and the rest of the children are turkeys. When the farmer calls out "Turkey," all the other children must go "Gobble, gobble." Using the sounds, the farmer tries to catch a turkey. When a turkey is caught, then that person becomes the farmer.

Longer Projects

Older students will enjoy painting the ice cream spoons to get ready to use in the turkey craft. Use acrylic instead of spray paint. Allow plenty of time for the paint to dry before the students put the turkey together.

Tell Aloud

Sing the song *Turkey Feathers* from the book *Felt Board Fingerplays: With Patterns and Activities* by Liz Wilmes. Make different colors of feathers from flannel, pass them out, and have the children bring up their feathers when their color is mentioned in the song. This is good for teaching younger children colors.

Tell the draw-and-tell story *The Turkey Tale*, found in *Twenty Tellable Tales* by Margaret Reed MacDonald, page 90. A picture of a turkey appears as you tell the story.

Food

Make a cookie turkey by pulling apart an Oreo or a chocolate sandwich cookie and putting one side vertically into the icing of the other side so it's in an L shape (you might need extra frosting to make it stick better), adding a row of candy corn around the edge of the vertical cookie half for feathers, and adding a candy kiss and red hot on the bottom cookie for the head and wattle.

Tips

Make flannel turkeys or finger puppets to count down with when saying the rhyme *Five Little Turkeys*, and don't forget to make a little red hen.

The song *Turkey Hunting We Will Go* is written for the book *A Turkey for Thanksgiving*. Hold up hand puppets or stick puppets during the verses while singing the song.

Program 35

VEGETABLE SOUP

Vegetable stories give you lots of choices. Whether you are planting vegetables in your garden, cooking with them, or hearing stories of vegetables that have grown to gigantic size or run away, you'll always have a variety of vegetables and stories to choose from.

Storytimes . . .

1. Rhymes and Songs

The Big Garden

Planting Time

I'm Planting My Garden

2. Storytime Picks

Brave Potatoes by Toby Speed

The Carrot Seed by Ruth Krauss

Cucumber Soup by Vickie Leigh Krudwig

Enormous Potato by Aubrey Davis

Growing Vegetable Soup by Lois Ehlert

Mrs. McNosh and the Great Big Squash by Sarah Weeks

No More Vegetables! by Nicole Rubel

Rabbit Food by Susanna Gretz

3. Crafty Corner

Vegetable Refrigerator Magnets

. . . Plus

4. Games

Veggie Guess

5. Longer Projects

Start a Garden

Mr. Potato Head

6. Tell Aloud

Jack and the Beanstalk

Stone Soup

7. Food

Vegetable Soup

Vegetables and Dip

8. Tips

STORYTIMES . . .

Rhymes and Songs

The Big Garden

Tune: Old McDonald

The farmer planted a big, big garden, E-I-E-I-O.
and in this garden was a big, big potato, E-I-E-I-O.
With a mash, mash here and a mash, mash there;
here a mash; there a mash; *(do motions)* everywhere a mash, mash.
The farmer planted a big, big garden, E-I-E-I-O.

The farmer planted a big, big garden, E-I-E-I-O.
and in this garden was a big, big carrot, E-I-E-I-O.
With a crunch, crunch here and a crunch, crunch there;
here a crunch, there a crunch; everywhere a crunch, crunch.
The farmer planted a big, big garden, E-I-E-I-O.

The farmer planted a big, big garden, E-I-E-I-O.
and in this garden was a big, big turnip, E-I-E-I-O.
With a pull, pull, here and a pull, pull, there;

here a pull, there a pull, everywhere a pull,
    pull.
The farmer planted a big, big garden, E-I-
    E-I-O.

The farmer planted a big, big garden, E-I-
    E-I-O.
and in this garden was a big, big bean, E-I-
    E-I-O.
With a snap, snap, here and a snap, snap,
    there;
here a snap, there a snap, everywhere a snap,
    snap.
The farmer planted a big, big garden, E-I-
    E-I-O.

The farmer planted a big, big garden, E-I-
    E-I-O.
and in this garden was a big, big onion, E-I-
    E-I-O.
With a boo hoo here and a boo hoo there;
here a boo, there a boo, everywhere a boo
    hoo.
The farmer planted a big, big garden, E-I-
    E-I-O.
(Add other vegetables as desired)

Planting Time

Tune: Here We Go Looby Loo

Here we go planting beans.
Here we go planting corn.

Here we go planting peas.
We're out in the sun so bright.

Here we go weeding here.
Here we go weeding there.
Here we go weeding here.
We're weeding with all of our might.

Now we water our beans.
Now we water our corn.
Now we water our peas.
We're watering with all of our might.

Here we go gathering beans.
Here we go gathering corn.
Here we go gathering peas.
Our garden is such a delight.
*(Make motions such as planting, pulling,
    etc.)*

I'm Planting My Garden *(A Rhyme)*

Chorus:
I'm planting my garden,
And I don't know what to do.
I'm planting my garden,
And I need some help from you.
*(Ask children for suggestions on what to
    plant)*

Storytime Picks

Brave Potatoes by Toby Speed, 2000. Potatoes escape from a county fair and after being pursued by a chef looking for potatoes, they rescue all the other vegetables trapped in his restaurant.

The Carrot Seed by Ruth Krauss, 1988. A boy believes his carrot seed will come up, even if no one else thinks so.

Cucumber Soup by Vickie Leigh Krudwig, 1998. In this version of the Big Turnip (also called the Enormous Turnip), insects join together to pull up a cucumber.

Enormous Potato by Aubrey Davis, 1998. In a new version of the classic "Enormous Turnip," everyone must help pull up the biggest potato in town.

Growing Vegetable Soup by Lois Ehlert, 1987. From garden to bowl, this book shows how vegetables grow and how soup is made.

Mrs. McNosh and the Great Big Squash by Sarah Weeks, 2000. Her squash is so big that Mrs. McNosh doesn't know what to do with it.

No More Vegetables! by Nicole Rubel, 2002. A little girl doesn't want to eat vegetables until she starts helping in the garden and watching how the vegetables grow.

Rabbit Food by Susanna Gretz, 1999. A little rabbit is a picky eater and does not like typical rabbit food.

Crafty Corner

Vegetable Refrigerator Magnets

Materials: Craft foam in vegetable colors (red, green, yellow, orange, brown), wiggle eyes, black marker, and magnetic strips.

Instructions:

1. Precut vegetable shapes for younger children *(patterns on pages 181–183)*.
2. Glue the stems and tops together, and then add the wiggle eyes.
3. Draw a mouth with the markers.
4. Glue a magnet strip to the back.

Alternatives: Use colored card stock or construction paper instead of the craft foam. Make a stick puppet instead of a refrigerator magnet. Glue a clothes pin on the back so it will hold papers.

Figure 35-1. Vegetable Refrigerator Magnets

. . . PLUS

Games

Veggie Guess

Put different vegetables in a box or bag where they cannot be seen. Then have the children reach in, feel the vegetable, and try to guess what it is. Bring some unusual and uncommon vegetables.

Longer Projects

Start a garden and plant vegetable seeds so the children can see different vegetables as they grow. If you can't plant an outside garden, use Styrofoam cups, small clay pots, or some other type of containers. Or have the children plant their seeds in small containers and take them home so they can watch them grow. If you wrap the seeds in wet paper towels, they will sprout in advance so the children can see results sooner. Decorate small pots with paint or markers.

Bring real potatoes and let the children create their own Mr. Potato Head. Use wiggle eyes, pipe cleaners, foam craft sheets, or whatever you can think of to turn your potato into a person. Bring a real Mr. Potato Head and let the children take turns playing with it. Be sure to read the potato books *The Enormous Potato* and *Brave Potatoes*.

Tell Aloud

Make flannel story pieces and tell aloud the classic story of another really big vegetable, *Jack and the Beanstalk*.

Tell the story *Stone Soup*, but use real vegetables (or perhaps plastic or flannel ones), a spoon, and some type of pot. A Halloween witch cauldron works well. Pass out the vegetables and let the children bring them up and toss them into the pot.

Food

Make homemade vegetable soup from your favorite recipe or used canned. Bring different types of sliced vegetables and dip for the children to taste, or simply serve vegetable-flavored crackers.

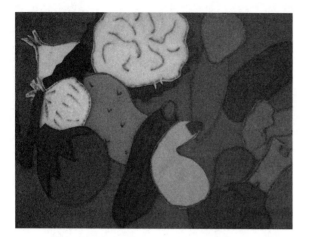

Figure 35-2. Vegetables (Flannel Board Examples)

Tips

An alternative to asking the children what to plant when reciting the rhyme *I'm Planting My Garden* would be to make flannel vegetables *(patterns on pages 181–183)* and ask the children what you are planting after you put up the flannel piece.

Combine the books *Growing Vegetable Soup* and *Cucumber Soup*, and then tell the story *Stone Soup*.

Compare some of the versions of *The Big Turnip*, such as *Enormous Potato*, *Cucumber Soup*, and *The Big Pumpkin* by Erica Silverman, and discuss how they are alike and different.

Part II
Storytimes . . . Plus Resources

Source A

STORIES AND SCRIPTS

A-1: THE NOISY ROCK (A DRAW-AND-TELL STORY BY PAT SNELL)

Once a boy went walking and found a rock. He touched the rock and it was warm sitting there in the sun.

Drawing 1

The little boy watched the rock. A butterfly landed on it and a tiny ant began to crawl up its side.

Drawing 2

Just then there was a little noise: "Rustle! Rustle!" It seemed to come from the rock, or perhaps under the rock. The little boy turned over the rock. Underneath the rock were a worm and a little black bug. Carefully the boy put the rock back in its place so as not to disturb the bug and the worm.

Drawing 3

The boy watched and listened. He saw a bird fly down to the ground near the rock. But the bird hadn't made the noise.

Drawing 4

The boy went looking for the sounds. He saw another bird. But the sound wasn't coming from that bird either.

Drawing 5

The boy walked a long way. As he walked the sound grew fainter.

Drawing 6

The boy knew he should turn back, so he turned around and started walking back toward the noise.

Drawing 7

The boy thought maybe the sound came from up on top of a nearby hill. He climbed the hill.

Drawing 8

The only thing he saw were lots of paths going down the side of the hill. The boy thought the paths had probably been made by animals. He hoped they weren't big scary animals. Now the sound turned to a grunting sound.

Drawing 9

The boy was a just a little bit afraid. So he hurried down the hill. At the bottom of the hill he saw the animal that was making the noise.

Drawing 10

It was a hungry armadillo looking for worms and bugs to eat.

A-2: WE'RE GOING ON A CHRISTMAS TREE HUNT (BY KAY LINCYCOMB)

Chorus:
We're going on a Christmas tree hunt.
Why don't you come too?
We'll hike into the dark, dark woods. *(Pat hands on knees as if walking)*
I'm not afraid, are you? *(Point to yourself and nod head no, point to audience)*

Let's go out the door *(Do actions)* and pick up our saw.
Now open the gate *(Squeak)*, and close the gate.
Now let's hike toward the woods. *(Pat knees again)*

(Repeat chorus)

We're in the woods, and we've come to a patch of deep deep snow.

We can't go around it, can't go over it, can't go under it.
We'll have to go through it.
(Move hands, and lean forward as if pushing aside snow)
We're through the deep snow. *(Pat hands again)*

(Repeat chorus)

Now, we've come to a pond that is frozen solid.
We can't go around it, can't go over it, can't go under it.
We'll have to go on top of it. *(Slide hands back and forth as if sliding on ice)*
Woo! It's slick.
We're over the frozen ice. *(Pat hands)*

(Repeat chorus)

We've come to a large and high snowdrift.
We can't go through it, can't go over it, can't go under it.
We'll have to go around it.
Let's run *(Pat hands very quickly, lean sideways)*
Half way around now. *(Pat hands very quickly, lean toward the other side)*
We are around the snowdrift at last. *(Pat hands)*

(Repeat chorus)

We've come to a bottom of a tall tall mountain.
We can't go around it, can't go through it, can't go under it.
We'll have to go over it. *(Pat hands, lifting high up as if climbing)*
We've come to the top at last.

Look at all the trees. *(Hands over eyes, look around)*
Let's walk through the forest and look for the best one. *(Pat hands)*
Look there beside that cave. *(Point)*
That's the perfect tree for our house. It's so full and beautiful.
Let's go closer. *(Pat hands, then stop and look up)* It's perfect.
What's that noise in the cave? *(Hand by ear)*

Let's go in and see. *(Pat hands slowly)*
It's dark in here; I can't see anything. *(Look around again)*
It's smelly in here. *(Hold nose)*
What's that big shape right there? *(Reach hand out and act if you are feeling something)*
It feels furry. *(Feel again, higher)*
It feels big.
It's growling!
It's a BEAR! *(Yell)* Run! *(Pat hands very fast)*
Out of the cave. *(Pat hands very fast as if running)*
Down the hill. *(Pat hands fast lifting high, as if running down hill)*
Around the large and high snowdrift. *(Pat hands quickly, lean to one side, then the other)*
Over the ice. *(Sliding hands quickly)* Woo!
Through the patch of deep snow. *(Move hands quickly as if digging snow)*
Open the gate. *(Make squeak noise)* Close the gate *(Squeak again)*
Throw down the saw. *(Do motion)*
Open the front door, close the door. *(Do motions)*
(Breathe loudly) I think I'll just get my tree at Wal-Mart this year. *(Point to audience)*
How about you?

A-3: ONCE UPON AN ACCIDENT, A FAIRY TALE FILLED WITH PERIL (BY KAY LINCYCOMB)

Characters:

Narrator: Nurse Muffet *(Little Miss Muffet dressed as a nurse)*
Big Bad Wolf
Pigs *(Optional one to three)*
Little Old Woman Who Swallowed a Fly
Goldilocks
Bear *(Optional one to three)*
Humpty Dumpty *(break apart if available)*
Little Red Riding Hood
Grandmother
Spider

Props:

Sign labeled "Far and Away Hospital"
Brick house painted on poster board

Big pot for wolf to fall in

Bowl and spoon labeled "Curds and Whey"

Bottle of burn ointment and bandage

Pan *(For old lady to throw up in)*

Beanbag props of animals that old lady swallows *(These usually come with old lady puppet)*

Picture or poster of three little bears' house *(You may use the same poster)*

Band-Aids and headache medication for Humpty

Basket for Red Riding Hood and a variety of junk food and healthy things to put in it

Plastic syringe for Red's shot

Grandmother's bed *(Use the same bed as for the Three Bears)*

Scenes:

I. *(Burns)* Big Bad Wolf and the Three Little Pigs

II. *(Stomachaches)* Little Old Woman Who Swallowed a Fly

III. *(Injuries/Broken Bones)* Goldilocks and the Three Bears

IV. *(Injuries/Headaches)* Humpty Dumpty

V. *(Colds and Flu/StrangerDanger/Dental Health/Healthy Lifestyle)* Little Red Riding Hood

Scene I (Music plays until Nurse Muffet enters)

Nurse: *(Enters)* Hello, boys and girls, and welcome to the land of Far, Far, Away! My name is Nurse Muffet, and I work at the Far, Far Away Hospital. I teach our citizens about safety and good nutrition. *(Looking around and spotting someone)* Speaking of citizens, here comes one of our not-quite-so-upstanding citizens right now.

Big Bad Wolf: *(Comes onto set, looking around)*

Nurse: Mr. Big Bad Wolf, what are you up to, sneaking around like that?

Big Bad Wolf: *(Jumps as if startled)* Oh my! Why, hello there, Nurse Muffet. I am just out and about on my morning walk, on my way to breakfast. As you can see I am not bothering anyone. *(Turns toward audience)* Yet!

Nurse: Well, you had just better behave yourself, Mr. Big Bad. I don't want to see a single citizen coming in with bite marks. Do you hear?

Big Bad Wolf: Oh, don't worry about a thing, Nurse Muffet; you won't see anyone with bite marks from me. *(Nurse leaves, wolf turns to audience)* That's because I am going to eat them ALL up. There won't be anything left to see. No evidence! *(Laughs wickedly)*

Wolf: Now, where was I? Oh, yes! I just blew down two little pigs' houses, one of straw and one of sticks, but they got away before I caught them. Now I am on my way to the third pig's house. That's where they are all hiding. I want to eat them ALL!

(Brick house goes up, pig or pigs behind it)

Big Bad Wolf: Well, there it is right now. *(Knocks and shouts)* Mr. Pig, Mr. Pig, let me come in!

Pigs: Not by the hair of our chinny chin chins!

Big Bad Wolf: Then I'll huff and I'll puff until I blow your house in. *(Blows loudly)* Oh, my! That brick house is really tough. I'll try again. Help me blow, boys and girls. *(Blows hard and long, ending in coughing and panting)*. Oh dear, I've never been unable to blow down a house before. But I will not give up. They don't call me big and bad for nothing. *(Evil laughter)*

What shall I do? Could I break out the windows? *(Looks around and then up)* I know, I see a chimney; I'll climb up the house and slide down the chimney. If Santa can do it, so can I, because I'm a lot thinner than he is. *(Evil laughter while leaving set)*

Pigs: *(Goes onto stage and pushes a large pot back on)* Pant! Pant! When the wolf slides down the chimney, he will land in this pot of boiling water. I sure hope this works, and then we will have him for dinner instead of the other way around. *(Pig or pigs giggle, and exit)*

Big Bad Wolf: *(Voice from off stage)* Here I comeeeeee! *(Falls from top of stage into or behind pot and jumps back up screaming)* Owwwwwwwwwwww! Hottttttttttttttttttttttt! *(Runs off stage)*

Pigs: It worked! We are safe at last. *(Giggle and exit)*

(House and pot removed)

Nurse Muffet: *(Enters, eating from bowl labeled "Curds and Whey" in large letters)*

Wolf: *(Runs back on stage again, screaming)* Nurse Muffet! Nurse Muffet! My butt is burned! My butt is burned! Ouch! Ouch! Ouch! Ouch!

Nurse: *(Puts down bowl)* Oh my goodness, Mr. Wolf. What have you done? Hold still, and let me help. *(Pulls out burn ointment, puts it on the wolf, and ties a bandage around his tail)*

Big Bad Wolf: Ahhhhhhhh! That feels sooooooo much better now!

Nurse: Mr. Wolf, you were very careless. You must be careful around hot things, because burns can be very serious and very painful injuries.

Big Bad Wolf: You are right, Nurse Muffet, burns do NOT feel good. Thank you so much, Nurse Muffet. I will not go down any more chimneys. *(Walks off stage)* Ouch! Ouch! Ouch!

Nurse: Mr. Wolf certainly found out the hard way to be careful of hot objects on the stove or fire.

Scene II *(From off stage, loud moaning)*

Nurse: *(Looks up)* Oh my goodness! What is that awful noise?

(Loud moaning again)

Nurse: Who's there? *(Turns toward audience)* Do you think it's a ghost?

(Even louder moaning)

Nurse: Who is it? Do you think it's a monster? You come out now! I have a weapon. *(Picks up spoon and holds it like a weapon)*

(Enters Old Lady Who swallowed a Fly, moaning and holding stomach)

Nurse: Oh my! It's the Old Lady! What is the matter?

Old Lady: My tummy hurts so badly. Please help me, Nurse Muffet!

Nurse: Whatever have you been eating, Old Lady?

Old Lady: Well, it all started when I swallowed a fly.

Nurse: You swallowed a fly? Oh my! Oh my!

Old Lady: *(Speaking Slowly)* Yes, I swallowed a fly, and I could just cry. Uh-oh! *(Begins making throwing-up sounds, tosses fly into audience)*

Nurse: Oops! *(Puts a pan or pail beside old lady)* Can someone in the audience bring that fly up and put it in this bucket? *(Waits for child to bring up fly)* Thank you so much! *(Acts as if grossed out)* Yuck! That was not a good choice to eat, Old Lady. Do you feel better now?

Old Lady: Well, not really, because then, you see, I swallowed a spider.

Nurse: A spider! A spider! I don't like spiders. Why did you swallow a spider?

Old Lady: I swallowed a spider to catch the fly.

Nurse: *(To audience)* That spider must be wiggling and wiggling and tickling inside her.

Old Lady: Oh my, oh my, I could just cry! Uh-oh! *(Makes throwing up sounds again, and tosses spider into audience)*

Nurse: I simply cannot tolerate spiders. Can someone please bring the spider up and put it in the bucket? Oh, thank you so much for your help. My, oh my, that wasn't a good thing to eat, Old Lady. Do you feel better now?

Old Lady: No, not really, because then, you see, I swallowed a bird.

Nurse: A bird? But that's absurd! *(To audience)* She swallowed the bird to catch the spider, which wiggled and wiggled and tickled inside her. And she swallowed the spider to catch the fly.

Old Lady: Oh my, I could just cry! Uh-oh! *(Makes throwing up sounds and tosses the bird)*

Nurse: Can someone in the audience bring up that bird and put it in the bucket? Thank you so much. My, oh my, that wasn't a good thing to eat, Old Lady. Do you feel better now?

Old Lady: Well, not really, because then I swallowed a cat!

Nurse: You swallowed a cat! Imagine that! She swallowed a cat to catch the bird. She swallowed the bird to catch the spider that wiggled and wiggled and tickled inside her. She swallowed the spider to catch the fly.

Old Lady: Oh my, I could just cry! Uh-oh! *(Makes throwing up sounds and tosses the cat)*

Nurse: My, oh my, that wasn't a good thing to eat, Old Lady. Do you feel better NOW?

Old Lady: Not really, because then I swallowed a dog!

Nurse: *(Slaps head in frustration)* You swallowed a dog! My, what a hog to swallow a dog. She swallowed a dog to catch the cat. She swallowed the cat to catch the bird. She swallowed the bird to catch the spider that wiggled and wiggled and tickled inside her. She swallowed the spider to catch the fly.

Old Lady: Oh my, I could just cry! Uh-oh! *(Makes throwing up sounds and tosses the dog)*

Nurse: Can someone in the audience bring up that dog and put it in the bucket? Thank you so much. My, oh my, that wasn't a good thing to eat, Old Lady. Surely you are starting to feel better now?

Old Lady: Not really, you see, because then I swallowed a cow.

Nurse: A COW! *(Looks at audience, puts hand over eyes, shakes head, and then looks up)* WOW! She swallowed a cow to catch the dog. She swallowed the dog to catch the cat. She swallowed the cat to catch the bird. She swallowed the bird to catch the spider that wiggled and wiggled and tickled inside her. She swallowed the spider to catch the fly.

Old Lady: Oh my, I could just cry! Uh-oh! *(Makes throwing up sounds and tosses cow into the audience)*

Nurse: Can someone in the audience bring up that cow and put it in the bucket? Thank you so much. My, oh my, that wasn't a good thing to eat, Old Lady. Is that everything? There couldn't be anything else in your tummy, now, could there?

Old Lady: Not really, because then you see I swallowed a horse.

Nurse: *(Throws up hands and screams)* AHHHHHHH! You swallowed a horse. That made you sick, of course! She swallowed a horse to catch the cow. She swallowed a cow to catch the dog. She swallowed the dog to catch the cat. She swallowed the cat to catch the bird. She swallowed the bird to catch the spider that wiggled and wiggled and tickled inside her. She swallowed the spider to catch the fly.

Old Lady: Oh my, I could just cry! Uh-oh! *(Makes throwing up sounds and tosses horse)*

Nurse: Can someone in the audience bring up that horse and put it in the bucket? Thank you so much. Yuck! My, oh my, that wasn't a good thing to eat, Old Lady. NOW do you feel better?

Old Lady: Oh yes, I feel MUCH better now. I think I'll go have supper. *(Leaves stage)*

Nurse: *(Shakes head)* You must be careful with what you eat. Eating too much or the wrong things can give you tummyaches. *(Bucket stays on side of stage)*

Scene III

Goldilocks: *(Singing from off stage)* La la la la la!

Nurse: Well, look who we have here. It's Goldilocks. Hello, Goldie. Where are you off to?

Goldilocks: *(Comes on stage)* Hello, Nurse Muffet. I have just been out playing all morning.

Nurse: Well, have a good day, Goldie, and don't wander too far from your home. *(Exits stage)*

Goldilocks: Oh, don't worry about me, Nurse Muffet, *(Singing)* la la la la la la. Wow, I am sure getting tired and hungry. I have gone an awful long way from home. Way too far to go back for a snack and a rest. *(Looks around)*

(Bear's house comes up)

Goldilocks: I wonder who lives in that pretty little cottage over there. I think I'll go knock on the door; maybe they'll let me come in and rest a bit. *(Knocks, someone off stage makes knocking sound)* HELLO! *(Knocks again)* Maybe they just can't hear me. *(Turns to audience)* I'll just try the door. *(Reaches out to try the door)* Hmmmmmm. The door isn't locked. I wonder if I should just go in and call again. Maybe. What do you in the audience think? Should I go in or not? I am so hungry and tired, I think I will just go in. *(House goes down. Goldie walks off stage and then back on.)*

Goldilocks: *(Goes to the bucket on stage that contains what the Old Lady threw up, and looks in it)* Look at that. Someone has left their breakfast out. If it just sits here it will get cold and be wasted. I'm sooooo hungry. If I eat it, I will keep it from being wasted, and they will appreciate my thoughtfulness. *(Puts her head in bucket, and takes a bit)* Hmmmmm, it's not too bad. *(Puts her head back in the bucket and eats quickly and messily, spilling a few animals out)* Oops! Looks like I got carried away and ate the whole thing. *(Burps, then giggles)* You know, I'm starting to feel a little sick. I wonder what was in that porridge? It seems to be giving me a tummyache. I think I need to lie down for a while.

(Exits room; put up bed)

Goldilocks: *(Enters as if coming upstairs)* I wonder what is up here. Look at that lovely bed over there. I'm so tired. Surely if there were someone here, they would offer me a place to rest. *(Goes to bed and lies down)* It feels so soft. *(Starts to make snoring sounds)*

Bear: *(One to three bears can be used. They come in to room.)* Look, there is someone in one of our beds! It must be the person who ate our food. *(Moves close to bed and shouts)* WHO'S THAT SLEEPING IN OUR BED?

Goldilocks: *(Wakes up, sits up in bed, looks at bear, and then screams)* AYYYYYYYYYY! IT'S A BEAR!

Bear: AYYYYYYYYYYYYYY! IT'S A HUMAN!

Goldilocks: AYYYYYYYYY! *(Begins to run around room)*

Bear: AYYYYYYYYY! *(Runs off stage)*

Goldilocks: How will I ever get out of here? What shall I do? *(Looks back and forth around room)* There's a window. *(Runs and jumps out window, by jumping off stage. From off stage comes a scream and a big thud or crash.)* Ohhhhhh!

Nurse: *(Enters stage, rolling bandages)* My, what a busy morning it's been—so many accidents.

Goldilocks: *(Limps back on)* Nurse Muffet, please help me. I fell out of a window and hurt my leg.

Nurse: Oh my! *(begins to wrap her leg in bandage)* How did you fall out of a window?

Goldilocks: *(Looks at audience)* Well, ahhh, well, maybe I kind of jumped a little.

Nurse: That was a very careless thing to do, Goldie. You could have been hurt very badly doing something like that. *(Finishes wrapping her leg)*

Goldie: You are right, Nurse Muffet; it was a careless thing to do. Thank you, Nurse Muffet. It feels so much better. *(Exits)*

Nurse: Now, don't go jumping from any more high places, young lady!

Scene IV

Humpty: *(Voice coming from above)* LOOK OUT BELOW! *(Humpty falls from top of stage, breaking apart if you use the break-apart puppet)* WHOAAAAAAAA!

Nurse: *(Covers head)* OH MY! Are you all right? *(Picks up Humpty and lays him onstage)*

Humpty: GROAN!

Nurse: It's Humpty Dumpty, isn't it? Oh dear, I see we have a problem. What ever happened to you, Mr. Dumpty?

Humpty: Well, you see, I was quite content just sitting on that wall, when suddenly a strong wind came, and I took a great big fall.

Nurse: *(Shakes head)* Oh dear me! There does seem to be some damage.

Humpty: I fear the king's horses and all the king's men do not have the skills to put me together again. So I come to you, Nurse, because of skills you aren't lacking. Please do something to keep my shell from more cracking.

Nurse: *(Puts Humpty back together and places a couple of bandages on him)* Now that's much better. How do you feel?

Humpty: Much better, Nurse Muffet, but my head hurts a little. And with MY head the pain goes from the top to my middle. *(Nurse Muffet points to top on head, and bottom of shell during this)*

Nurse: Well, here is some headache medication. Now take my advice and stay off walls. Now, go rest in your egg carton.

Humpty: Gratitude you have earned from this happy and round old bloke. You saved my shell and kept me from becoming just runny yolk. *(Goes off stage)*

Nurse: Some of those poetic sorts are quite a strange bunch.

Scene V

Nurse: Well, who is that walking down the lane? It's Little Red Riding Hood.

Red: (*Enters stage carrying a basket*) Hello, Nurse Muffet. How are you today?

Nurse: I'm quite well, Miss Hood, and how are you and your family? I don't think your family has been in for their flu shots yet.

Red: I'm fine, Nurse Muffet, but unfortunately my grandma is ill. She waited too late to get her flu shot.

Nurse: That's too bad. What's in your basket?

Red: It's good stuff like donuts, chocolate chip cookies, and Coke, to make my grandma feel better.

Nurse: Oh my, that is not good food; it is very unhealthy food. (*Takes out junk food*) Here, take these things to help your grandma get better and stay healthy. (*Puts miscellaneous healthy things in basket*)

Nurse: Now, can you carry all that?

Red: Well, it's very heavy, but I met a new friend along the way, and he is going to help me. (*Turns to look for friend*) Well, he was here just a minute ago, but I don't see him now. Where did he go? He was such a friendly person, and the poor thing had been in a terrible accident. Burned the hair right off his butt in a house fire. (*Giggles*)

Nurse: Oh my, Little Red, you should be more careful about talking to strangers. That was the Big Bad Wolf, and he was burned while trying to eat the Three Little Pigs. You stay away from him. Be aware of stranger danger, my dear!

Red: Oh! My! I just didn't think. Thank you so much for the warning, Nurse Muffet. I will be more careful talking with strangers. And this was a very strange creature indeed.

Nurse: Always use caution, my dear. Say, let me give you your flu shot before you go!

Red: No! I don't want to. I'm afraid it will hurt a lot.

Nurse: It'll be over in a minute.

Red: (*Hides her eyes*) I may scream! (*Nurse gives Red the shot*) It's gonna hurt! Tell me when you do it. I don't want it. I'm gonna scream. Tell me when you do it.

Nurse: Red, (*Taps her on shoulder*) Red, I already gave you your flu shot.

Red: (*Uncovers eyes and looks at arm*) Oh! Well, that wasn't so bad after all. Certainly better than having the flu. I think I'll get one every year. Well, I must run now. Bye, Nurse Muffet. (*Leaves stage*)

Nurse: Be careful, Red! (*Leaves stage*)

Wolf: (*Brick wall up, wolf enters and talks to audience*) This has been the worst day; I'm still trying to get my breakfast. But I have another plan now. I'm going to sneak in and scare Little Red's grandma off, then hide in her bed, and take Red's basket of goodies for myself. (*Wolf exits, wall down, bed up, wolf comes back on*)

Wolf: (*Looking around*) Where is that grandma? She's not here. Oh well, one less person to worry about. I won't have to scare her off after all; I'll just jump in the bed and hide. (*Gets in bed and covers up*) I'm so tired; this bed really feels good. (*Snoring sounds*)

Grandma: (*Enters*) Now who is that sleeping in MY bed? (*Yanks off covers*)

Wolf: Yikes! (*Jumps out of bed*)

Grandma: Who are you?

Wolf: I'm a scary wolf! ROAR!

Grandma: Ooh-wee! Mr. Wolf, your breath smells bad. *(Fans her face)* What have you been eating?

Wolf: Good stuff like candy, and cookies, and pigs. And I came here to get more.

Grandma: That's a terrible diet. I bet you are the one that ate the gingerbread house that those poor little children, Hansel and Gretel, were accused of doing.

Wolf: Wellllll! Maybe I did it. *(Turns toward audience)* But you can't prove it.

Grandma: I bet you don't even clean your teeth and floss. That would help your bad breath, and I bet you don't eat right either. *(Pushes wolf)*

Wolf: *(Stumbles)* Hey, stop that. I'm the bully here!

Grandma: How do you think I got over the flu so fast? I eat right and exercise, so I am strong and healthy.

Wolf: I'm strong and healthy too.

Grandma: No, you're not. Just look how weak you are. *(Throws wolf off stage)*

Wolf: *(From off stage)* Ahhhhhhh! *(Loud thump or crash)*

Grandma: Silly wolf. Guess I'll go wait for my granddaughter to come. She should be here any minute. *(Leaves stage)*

Wolf: *(Comes back on stage and looks around)* Is that scary woman gone yet? This has been a VERY bad day. I think I'll just go get my breakfast at McDonald's. *(Exits)*

Nurse: *(Enters stage)* That silly wolf. *(Shakes head)* Well, I hope all our citizens of Far Far Away and all of you in our audience have learned some pointers to keep yourself safe and healthy. And be sure to stay away from Mr. Wolf and other strange creatures.

(Spider drops from a string down from the top of the stage, getting lower and lower as nurse is talking)

Nurse: *(Sees spider)* AAAAAAAAAAA! *(Screams and runs off stage)*

Spider: Nurse Muffet? Nurse Muffet, come back! Gee, I just wanted to borrow her hairdryer. I had a little accident in the water spout and am all wet.

(Music starts to play and spider leaves)

(If you wish, all the puppets can appear and take a bow as the music plays)

The End

A-4: GOING ON A TRAIL RIDE (A PARTICIPATION STORY BY KAY LINCYCOMB)

Chorus:
Clip, Clop, Clip, Clop! *(Pat hands on legs as you speak for beat)*
I'm going on a trail ride. That's what I'm going to do.
I'm going on a trail ride. You come too. *(Point to audience)*

We're at the gate. Open the gate. Squeak! *(Do motions like you are opening a door)*
Now close the gate. Squeak! *(Do motions)*
Let's get on our horse *(Lift foot)* and ride on the trail. *(Pat hands on knees)*

(Repeat chorus)
We've come to a field of tall prairie grass,
Can't go over it, can't go around it, we'll have to go through it.
Swish, Swish, Swish, Swish! *(Move hands as if parting grass)*
Now we're through it.

(Repeat chorus)
We come to a growth of tall and wide cactus,
Can't go over it, can't go through it, better go around it.
Clip, clop, clip, clop! *(Lean far to one side, then the other, as you pat your knees)*

Now we're around it.

(Repeat chorus)
Now we've come to a deep pond,
Can't go around it, can't go over it, better
swim through it.
Splash, splash, splash, splash! *(Make dog-paddle motions)* Now we're through it.

Now we've come to a tall hill, *(Look up)*
Can't go through it, Can go around it, better
go over it.

Clip, clop, clip, clop! *(Raise hands high as with effort climbing)*
Now we're at the top.

It's so pretty up here, let's look around. *(Put hands over eyes)*
Look at those big rocks over there! *(Point)*
Is there something there? *(Shrug)* Let's go
over and see. *(Hands)*
Let's get down from our horse *(Lift foot)*
And walk over to the rocks. *(Walk in place)*
Let's look closely at this little hole *(Lean forward)*
Let's reach in. *(Put out arm and move fingers)*

I feel something that's furry, and it smells
bad too. *(Hold nose)*
I hear something. *(Hand to ear)*
It's a COYOTE! *(Yell)*
LETS GET OUT OF HERE!
(Do all motions very quickly as if running)
Run back to our horse! *(Run in place)*
Jump on. *(Lift feet)* Ride fast. *(Pat hands)*
Clip, Clop, Clip, Clop!
Down the hill. Clip, Clop, Clip, Clop!
Through the deep pond. *(Dog paddle)*
Splash, splash, splash, splash!
Around the cactus. *(Lean)* Clip, Clop, Clip,
Clop!
Through the prairie grass. *(Move hands)*
Swish, swish, swish, swish!
We're to the gate. Jump off your horse.
(Jump)
Open the gate. *(Do motions)* Squeak! Close
the gate. Squeak!
We're safe at the ranch. *(Give big sigh of relief)*
What an exciting trail ride!
I sure had fun! *(Point to self)* Did you?
(Point to audience)

A-5: ADVENTURES OF GARY GHOST (A FELT BOARD HALLOWEEN STORY REVISED BY KAY LINCYCOMB (ORIGINAL AUTHOR UNKNOWN)

Directions

In advance make ten flannel ghosts from pattern using the colors from the story. Make two dots with a marker on each ghost for eyes. On one side of the white ghost draw a smiling mouth, and on the opposite side draw a frown. On the rest of the ghosts draw a frown on one side only.

As you tell the story, start with the white ghost with the frown side up, and place the other ghosts directly on top of the white one as the story is told.

When the story ends, quickly flip the white ghost around to reveal the side with the smile.

When all the ghosts are layered on the flannel board, they get a little bit heavy, so you might want to keep your hand on them or put a tiny piece of Velcro on the back of the ghosts.

Story

It was Halloween night and all the ghosts were getting ready to go out. Their white sheets were clean and they were happy and ready to go, except for Gary Ghost.

Gary was unhappy. Gary was tired of being just like everyone else.

Gary complained, "I am tired of always being the color white, just like all the other ghosts. I want to be different, so everyone will notice me."

As soon as all the other ghosts had left, Gary had an idea. He could paint himself another color, and then he would be different from all the rest of the ghosts. Gary thought a long time about what color he should be.

Gary said, "Apples are red, and lollipops are too. Red is a wonderful color. I think I will be red." So he painted himself red. *(Make painting motions, and place the red ghost on top of the white one)*

Can you think of other things that are red?

Gary looked at himself and was very pleased, so he decided to go out for Halloween. He left the house and walked down the street. *(Make motions of opening squeaky door and shutting door and walk in place)*

(This part is repeated, each time substituting the person or thing and the color) As Gary walked, the moon *(point up)* in the sky looked down and saw Gary. The moon said, "Whoever heard of a red ghost?"

Gary said, "I do not want to be a white ghost like all the others, so I painted myself red."

The moon said, "Well, if you are going to be another color, you should be yellow like me. Yellow is the best color of all. I am yellow; the sun is too. And lots of flowers are yellow. You should be yellow."

Can you think of other things that are yellow?

Gary thought about it and decided he wanted to be yellow, so he turned around and walked back to his house *(Make motions of walking and opening and closing the squeaky door)* and painted himself yellow *(make painting motions, then put yellow flannel ghost directly on top of red one)*.

Gary looked at himself and was very pleased, so he once again left the house and began walking down the street. *(Repeat motions)*

(Repeat the story again but substituting the following and the color each time)

Soon Gary met *(fill in the person or thing)* . . .

The *(person or thing)* said, "Whoever heard of a *(fill in the color)* ghost?" . . .

Gary said, "I do not want to be a white ghost like all the others, so I painted myself *(fill in the color)*."

The *(fill in the person or thing)* said, "Well, if you are going to be another color, you should be *(fill in the color)* like *(the speaker)*."

(Fill in the color) is the best color of all . . . *(repeat with the colors below)*

Can you think of other things that are *(fill in the color)*?

Gary thought about it and decided he wanted to be *(fill in the color)*, so he turned around and walked back to his house *(make motions)* and painted himself *(fill in the color)*.

(Put the matching color flannel on top)

Gary looked at himself and was very pleased, so once again he left the house and began walking down the street. *(Repeat motions)*

Verses to Add:

. . . Soon he met a little girl in a blue dress, who was trick-or-treating.

The little girl said, "If you are going to be another color, you should be a blue ghost.

Blue is the color of my dress and is the color of my eyes. You should be blue."

. . . Soon Gary was getting tired and so he sat down to rest under a tree.

The tree said, "If you are going to be another color, you should be green.

Green is the color of my leaves, and the color of the grass. You should be green."

. . . And as he walked, suddenly an old witch flew by overhead.

The witch cackled and said, "If you are going to be another color, you should be black.

My clothes are black, and my pet cat is black. You should be black."

. . . Now Gary was very tired indeed. He passed by a fence, on which sat a big Jack-O-Lantern. The Jack-O-Lantern said, "If you are going to be another color, you should be orange. I am orange, and orange is the color of Halloween. You should be orange."

Ending, When Finished with Colors:

Gary was very tired, and walked very, very slowly down the street. Gary decided that he had better get going if he wanted any time to scare people, because it was getting very late. So Gary started to take off into the air *(try to jump)*, and found that he couldn't get off the ground because he was so heavy from all those layers of paint. Gary sat down and cried. *(Crying, "Boo! Hoo!")*

All of a sudden, he heard the voice of a wise old owl which had been sitting in the tree and watching Gary all night long. Mr. Owl said to him, "Gary, don't you know that everyone has their own special color that is just right for them? The special color for ghosts is white, and that is the best color for you."

Gary decided that Mr. Owl was right, so he hurried home *(quickly make motions of running and opening a door and make a squeaking sound)*

and he took a bar of soap *(make motions of washing)*

and washed off the layer of orange *(take off the orange felt ghost as Gary washes)*

and washed off the layer of black *(take off black ghost)*

and washed off the layer of green *(take off green ghost)*

and washed off the layer of blue *(take off blue ghost)*

and washed off the layer of yellow *(take off yellow ghost)*

and washed off the layer of red *(take off red ghost, and very quickly flip over the white ghost to show the smiling side)*.

Now Gary was a white Halloween ghost again, very happy. Off he flew, to join the other ghosts for a fun Halloween night.

There are many different versions of this story such as Scat the Cat; The Cat of Many Colors; and A Ghost Called Matt. This has been rewritten in my own words and shortened. Other colors may be added to the story if you wish.

A-6: BUBBADILLO (A PUPPET PLAY FOR STICK PUPPETS WRITTEN BY PAT SNELL)

Puppets: *(See patterns)*

1 armadillo, with blue bands on its back for Bubbadillo

1 armadillo with pink bands on its back for Sissydillo

1 larger armadillo for Mamadillo

(You may also use real puppets)

Props:

Leaflet

Paper phone on a stick or a toy phone

Narrator: Little Bubbadillo was the loneliest armadillo in the state of Texas.

Bubba: *(Whines)* I'm really lonesome.

Narrator: He didn't have any friends and his mamadillo worked all day at the local cannery processing fire ants to put in the cannery's chilidillo. School would be out soon and Bubba just hated the thought of being alone all day with nothing to do.

Bubba: *(Whining still)* I'm gonna be so bored and lonely with nothing to do.

Narrator: Then one day something happened at school that changed all that. Teacherdillo passed out leaflets about the summer programs at the local public library. Little Bubbadillo was so excited he ran all the way home.

Bubbadillo: *(Looks at leaflets and runs)*

Narrator: When Mamadillo came home from the cannery, he met her at the door.

(Bring up Mamadillo)

Bubba: *(Jumping up and down)* Mamadillo! Mamadillo! See here! See here! Look what's happening at the library this summer! Can I sign up? Please can I?

Mama: *May* I sign up, Bubbadillo! Let me see the flyer. My, it says here there will be puppet shows, a magician, and a clown. *(Change to reflect local events)* And it also says there will be a reading club. Let's call the library and find out more. *(Bring up telephone)* Hello. Will you tell me about your summer programs for children? I also want to know about your reading club.

Librarian: *(Offstage voice tells about summer reading or local events)*

Mama: My, that sounds so exciting, and it's all free! Thank you very much.

Bubba: Can I sign up, Mamadillo! Please, Mama?

Mama: *May* I, Bubbadillo. Yes, of course. Let me get my purse and we'll go down to the library right now.

Bubba: Oh, goody! Mamadillo, do you think they might be giving away coupons for beetle burgers?

Narrator: That was the summer little Bubbadillo's life was changed forever. He had so much fun at the library that he had plenty to do. And he checked out so many books to read at home, he wasn't bored at all. And best of all, he met a new friend at the library.

Sissy: Hi, my name's Sissydillo. Do you want to be friends?

Bubba: Wow! You're the prettiest giradillo I've every seen! My name's Bubbadillo. Can I carry your books?

Sissy: *May* I carry your books, Bubbadillo.

Bubba: Sure. You can carry my books and I'll carry yours.

Narrator: So Bubbadillo was never lonesome again, thanks to the library's summer programs for kidadillos. But, he never did learn to say "May I" instead of "Can I"!

Source B

BIBLIOGRAPHY OF SELECTED BOOKS

Aber, Linda Williams. 2002. *Grandma's Button Box*. New York: Kane Press.

Aliki. 1988. *How a Book Is Made*. New York: HarperTrophy.

Anglund, Joan Walsh. 2004. *The Cowboy's Christmas*. Kansas City, MO: Andrews McMeel.

Appelt, Kathi. 2004. *Bubba and Beau Meet the Relatives*. Orlando, FL: Harcourt.

Araki, Mie. 2004. *The Perfect Tail*. San Francisco, CA: Chronicle Books.

Arnosky, Jim. 2003. *Armadillo's Orange*. New York: Grosset and Dunlap.

Arnosky, Jim. 2005. *Coyote Raid in Cactus Canyon*. New York: G. P. Putnam's Sons.

Baker, Keith. 2004. *Meet Mr. and Mrs. Green*. San Diego, CA: Harcourt.

Baltuck, Naomi. 1993. *Crazy Gibberish and Other Story Stretches*. Hamden, CT: Linnet Books.

Bare, Colleen Stanley. 1993. *Guinea Pigs Don't Read Books*. London: Puffin Books.

Barner, Bob. 2001. *Dinosaur Bones*. San Francisco, CA: Chronicle Books.

Barry, Francis. 2004. *Duckie's Rainbow*. Cambridge, MA: Candlewick.

Barton, Byron. 1990. *Bones, Bones, Dinosaur Bones*. New York: HarperCollins.

Bateman, Teresa. 1999. *Leprechaun Gold*. New York: Holiday House.

Baurys, Florance. 1999. *A Spur for Christmas*. Houston, TX: Enchanted Rock.

Beaton, Clare. 2001. *There's a Cow in the Cabbage Patch*. Cambridge, MA: Barefoot Books.

Beaton, Clare. 2005. *Daisy Gets Dressed*. Cambridge, MA: Barefoot Books.

Bedford, David. 2002. *Healthy Wolf*. London: Little Tiger Press.

Bedford, David. 2004. *Copy Crocs*. Atlanta, GA: Peachtree Publishers.

Benfanti, Russell. 2002. *Hide Clyde*. New York: Ipicturebooks.

Berenzy, Alix. 2005. *Sammy the Classroom Guinea Pig*. New York: Henry Holt.

Bertram, Debbie. 2005. *The Best Time to Read*. New York: Random House Books for Young Readers.

Bloom, Suzanne. 2005. *A Splendid Friend Indeed*. Honesdale, PA: Boyds Mills.

Bock, Lee. 2003. *Oh, Crumps!* Green Bay, WI: Raven Tree Press.

Boniface, William. 2003. *Five Little Turkeys*. New York: Price Stern Sloan.

Bonnett-Rampersaud, Louise. 2001. *Polly Hopper's Pouch*. New York: Dutton Juvenile.

Boyce, Katie. 2003. *Hector the Hermit Crab*. New York: Bloomsbury Children's Books.

Brett, Jan. 1995. *Armadillo Rodeo*. New York: G. P. Putnam's Sons.

Brimner, Larry Dane. 1995. *Merry Christmas, Old Armadillo*. Honesdale, PA: Boyds Mills.

Brimner, Larry Dane. 2005. *Twelve Plump Cookies*. Chanhassen, MN: The Child's World.

Brown, Jo. 2002. *Where's My Mommy?* Wilton, CT: Tiger Tales.

Brown, Marc. 1994. *The Silly Tale Book*. Milwaukee, WI: Gareth Stevens Publishing.

Brown, Margaret Wise. 2001. *Two Little Trains*. New York: HarperCollins.

Brown, Margaret Wise. 2003. *Sheep Don't Count Sheep*. New York: Margaret K. McElderry Books.

Brown, Ruth. 1997. *The Big Sneeze*. New York: HarperTrophy.

Brown, Ruth. 2000. *Snail Trail*. New York: Crown Books for Young Readers.

Bruel, Nick. 2004. *Boing*. Brookfield, CT: Roaring Brook Press.

Bruss, Deborah. 2001. *Book! Book! Book!* New York: Arthur A. Levine Books.

Bunting, Eve. 1991. *A Turkey for Thanksgiving*. New York: Clarion.

Capucilli, Alyssa Satin. 1999. *Biscuit Finds a Friend*. New York: HarperCollins.

Capucilli, Alyssa Satin. 2003. *Biscuit Is Thankful*. New York: HarperFestival.

Carle, Eric. 1984. *The Mixed-Up Chameleon*. New York: HarperCollins.

Carle, Eric. 1991. *A House for Hermit Crab*. New York: Simon and Schuster Children's Publishing.

Carle, Eric. 1998. *Pancakes, Pancakes*. New York: Simon and Schuster Children's Publishing.

Carle, Eric. 2000. *Dream Snow*. New York: Philomel.

Carter, David A. 1999. *What's in My Pocket? A Pop-Up and Peek-In Book*. New York: Putnam.

Carter, David A. 2001. *Flapdoodle Dinosaurs (A Pop-Up)*. New York: Little Simon.

Cave, Kathryn. 2004. *That's What Friends Do*. New York: Hyperion.

Chen, Chih-Yuan. 2004. *Guji Guji*. La Jolla, CA: Kane/Miller Publishers.

Child, Lauren. 2000. *I Will Never NOT EVER Eat a Tomato*. Cambridge, MA: Candlewick.

Christelow, Eileen. 1991. *Five Little Monkeys Sitting in a Tree*. New York: Clarion.

Clark, Emma Chichester. 1999. *I Love You, Blue Kangaroo*. New York: Doubleday Books for Young Readers.

Cocca-Leffler, Maryann. 1990. *Wednesday Is Spaghetti Day*. New York: Scholastic.

Colborn, Mary Palenick. 2000. *Rainy Day Slug*. Seattle, WA: Sasquatch Books.

Cornette. 1999. *The Purple Coyote*. New York: Doubleday Books for Young Readers.

Cousins, Lucy. 1999. *Where Is Maisy?* Cambridge, MA: Candlewick.

Cousins, Lucy. 2000. *Where Are Maisy's Friends?* Cambridge, MA: Candlewick.

Cousins, Lucy. 2003. *Maisy's Rainbow Day*. Cambridge, MA: Candlewick.

Cousins, Lucy. 2005. *Maisy Goes to the Library*. Cambridge, MA: Candlewick.

Cowell, Cressida. 1999. *Little Bo-Peep's Library Book*. New York: Orchard Books.

Cox, Kenyon. 2005. *Mixed Beasts*. Toronto: Kids Can Press.

Crews, Donald. 2001. *Inside Freight Train*. New York: HarperFestival.

Cullen, Catherine Ann. 2001. *The Magical, Mystical, Marvelous Coat*. Boston: Little, Brown.

Curtis, Matt. 1998. *Six Empty Pockets*. New York: Children's Press.

Davis, Aubrey. 1998. *Enormous Potato*. Toronto: Kids Can Press.

Davis, Katie. 2003. *Mabel the Tooth Fairy and How She Got Her Job*. San Diego, CA: Harcourt Children's Books.

De Beer, Hans. 2004. *Oh No, Ono!* New York: North-South Books.

De Paola, Tomie. 1975. *Strega Nona*. New York: Simon and Schuster.

De Regniers, Beatrice Schenk. 2003. *What Did You Put in Your Pocket?* New York: HarperCollins.

DiPucchio, Kelly. 2005. *Dinosnores*. New York: HarperCollins.

Donaldson, Julia. 2004. *The Snail and the Whale*. New York: Dial Books for Young Readers.

Downey, Lynn. 2000. *The Flea's Sneeze*. New York: Henry Holt.

Dubanevich, Arlene. 1990. *Tom's Tale*. New York: Viking Children's Books.

Duke, Kate. 1998. *One Guinea Pig Is Not Enough*. New York: Dutton Juvenile.

Duke, Kate. 2000. *Twenty Is Too Many*. New York: Dutton Juvenile.

DuQuette, Keith. 2004. *Cock-a-Doodle Moooo! A Mixed-Up Menagerie*. New York: Grosset and Dunlap.

Durall, Kathy. 2005. *Three Bear's Christmas*. New York: Holiday House.

Edwards, Frank B. 1998. *Is the Spaghetti Ready?* New York: Firefly.

Edwards, Frank B. 1999. *Peek-a-boo at the Zoo*. Buffalo, NY: Firefly.

Edwards, Pamela D. 2001. *Slop Goes the Soup: A Noisy Warthog Word Book*. New York: Hyperion Books for Children.

Edwards, Pamela Duncan. 2005. *McGillycuddy Could!* New York: Katherine Tegen Books.

Ehlert, Lois. 1987. *Growing Vegetable Soup*. San Diego, CA: Harcourt Children's Books.

Ehlert, Lois. 1992. *Planting a Rainbow*. San Diego, CA: Harcourt Children's Books.

Ehlert, Lois. 1995. *Snowballs*. San Diego, CA: Harcourt Children's Books.

Elffers, Joost. 2005. *Food for Thought*. New York: Arthur A. Levine Books.

Ellis, Carey Armstrong. 2005. *Seymour Slug Starts School*. New York: Abrams Books for Young Readers.

Ernst, Lisa Campbell. 1998. *Stella Louella's Runaway Book*. New York: Simon and Schuster Children's Publishing.

Fearnley, Jan. 2000. *Mr. Wolf's Pancakes*. London: Little Tiger Press.

Fearnley, Jan. 2004. *Watch Out!* Cambridge, MA: Candlewick Press.

Fox, Mem. 2004. *Where Is the Green Sheep?* New York: Harcourt.

Fox, Mem. 2005. *Hunwick's Egg*. San Diego, CA: Harcourt.

Freedman, Michelle. 2005. *The Ravioli Kid*. Salt Lake City, UT: Gibbs Smith Publisher.

Freeman, Don. 1966. *A Rainbow of My Own*. New York: Viking Juvenile.

Freeman, Don. 1978. *A Pocket for Corduroy*. New York: Viking Juvenile.

Gay, Marie-Louise. 2005. *Stella, Queen of the Snow*. Toronto: Groundwood Books.

Gelman, Rita Golden. 1999. *More Spaghetti, I Say!* New York: Cartwheel.

Glaser, Tom. 1995. *On Top of Spaghetti*. Garden City, NY: Doubleday.

Gray, Kes. 2000. *The Get Well Soon Book, Good*

Wishes for Bad Times. Brookfield, Millbrook Press.

Gretz, Susanna. 1999. *Rabbit Food*. Cambridge, MA: Candlewick.

Handford, Martin. *Where's Waldo?* 1997. Cambridge, MA: Candlewick.

Harris, Lee. 1999. *Never Let Your Cat Make Lunch for You*. Berkeley, CA: Tricycle Press.

Hart, Marj. 1996. *Fold-and-Cut Stories and Fingerplays*. Belmont, CA: Fearon Teaching Aids.

Harvey, Paul. 1994. *Kathy's Pocket*. New York: Newbridge Educational Publishing.

Haskins, Lois. 2000. *Ducks in Muck*. New York: Random House Books for Young Readers.

Hayward, Linda. 2004. *I Am a Book*. Brookfield, CT: Millsbrook.

Heide, Florence Parry. 2003. *That's What Friends Are For*. Cambridge, MA: Candlewick Press.

Hennessy, B. G. 1992. *Corduroy's Christmas*. New York: Viking.

Higney, Michael-Gene. 2000. *Tales of Tails*. New York: Dutton Children's Books.

Hill, Eric. 1980. *Where's Spot?* New York: Putnam.

Hiscock, Bruce. 2001. *Coyote and Badger, Desert Hunters of the Southwest*. Honesdale, PA: Boyds Mills Press.

Hook, Jason. 2003. *Brian and Bob*. New York: Hyperion.

Hutchins, Pat. 1989. *The Doorbell Rang*. New York: Greenwillow.

Inkpen, Mike. 1995. *Where, Oh Where, Is Kipper's Bear?* New York: Red Wagon Books.

Inns, Christopher. 2001. *Next! Please*. Berkeley, CA: Tricycle Press.

Jackson, Alison. 1997. *I Know an Old Lady Who Swallowed a Pie*. New York: Dutton.

Jandl, Ernst. 2003. *Next Please*. New York: G.P. Putnam's Sons.

Johnston, Tony. 2004. *Ten Fat Turkeys*. New York: Scholastic.

Jorgensen, Gail. 1989. *Crocodile Beat*. New York: Simon and Schuster.

Kalan, Robert. 1996. *Moving Day*. New York: Greenwillow.

Ketteman, Helen. 2000. *Armadillo Tattletale*. New York: Scholastic.

Ketteman, Helen. 2004. *Armadilly Chili*. Morton Grove, IL: Albert Whitman.

Kimmel, Eric A. 1992. *I Took My Frog to the Library*. New York: Puffin.

Kirk, Daniel. 2004. *Lunchroom Lizard*. New York: G. P. Putnam's Sons.

Kirk, Daniel. 2004. *Snow Dude*. New York: Hyperion Books for Children.

Krauss, Ruth. 1988. *The Carrot Seed*. New York: Scholastic.

Krudwig, Vickie Leigh. 1998. *Cucumber Soup*. Golden, CO: Fulcrum.

Kuskin, Karla. 2004. *Under My Hood I Have a Hat*. New York: HarperCollins.

Larranaga, Ana Martin. 2000. *Woo! The Not-So-Scary-Ghost*. New York: Arthur A. Levine Books.

Lass, Bonnie. 2000. *Who Took the Cookies from the Cookie Jar?* New York: Little, Brown.

LeSieg, Theo. 1981. *The Tooth Book*. New York: Random House Books for Young Readers.

Leuck, Laura. 1999. *My Monster Mama Love Me So*. New York: HarperCollins.

Levine, Abby. 2000. *This Is the Turkey*. Martin Grove, IL: Albert Whitman.

Levitin, Sonia. 2001. *When Kangaroo Goes to School*. Flagstaff, AZ: Rising Moon.

Lewis, Kevin. 1999. *Chugga Chugga Choo Choo*. New York: Hyperion Books for Children.

Lewis, Paeony. 2005. *No More Cookies!* New York: Scholastic.

Lionni, Leo. 1994. *A Color of His Own*. New York: Alfred A. Knopf.

Lithgow, John. 2001. *Marsupial Sue*. New York: Simon and Schuster Children's Publishing.

Lobel, Arnold. 1970. *Frog and Toad Are Friends*. New York: HarperCollins.

London, Jonathan. 1992. *Froggy Gets Dressed*. New York: Viking.

London, Jonathan. 2001. *Froggy Eats Out*. New York: Viking Juvenile.

London, Jonathan. 2003. *Eat! Cried Little Pig*. New York: Dutton Juvenile.

Lowell, Susan. 1992. *Three Little Javelinas*. Flagstaff, AZ: Rising Moon.

Lund, Jillian. 1993. *Way Out West Lives a Coyote Named Frank*. New York: Dutton.

Lund, Jillian. 1999. *Two Cool Coyotes*. New York: Dutton.

MacDonald, Margaret Reed. 1986. *Twenty Tellable Tales*. New York: Wilson.

Mann, Pamela. 1995. *The Frog Princess*. Milwaukee, WI: Garth Stevens Publishers.

Many, Paul. 2002. *The Great Pancake Escape*. New York: Walker Books for Young Readers.

Markes, Julie. 2004. *Thanks for Thanksgiving*. New York: HarperCollins.

Marzollo, Jean. 1993. *I Spy*. New York: Cartwheel.

Marzollo, Jean. 1999. *Thanksgiving Cats*. New York: Scholastic.

Mayo, Gretchen. 1993. *Meet Tricky Coyote*. New York: Walker.

Mayo, Gretchen. 1993. *That Tricky Coyote*. New York: Walker.

McCourt, Lisa. 2004. *The Most Thankful Thing*. New York: Scholastic.

McDermott, Gerald. 1994. *Coyote*. San Diego, CA: Harcourt Children's Books.

McDonald, Megan. 1993. *Is This a House for Hermit Crab?* New York: Orchard.

McGinty, Alice B. 2002. *Ten Little Lambs.* New York: Dial Books for Young Readers.

McGuirk, Leslie. 2003. *Snail Boy.* Cambridge, MA: Candlewick Press.

McMullan, Kate. Various dates. *Fluffy the Classroom Guinea Pig (Series).* New York: Cartwheel Books.

McNaughton, Colin. 1996. *Oops!* San Diego, CA: Harcourt Brace.

Meade, Holly. 1998. *John Willy and Freddy McGee.* Tarrytown, NY: Marshall Cavendish.

Middleton, Charlotte. 2003. *Do You Still Love Me?* Cambridge, MA: Candlewick.

Milgrim, David. 2003. *Thank You, Thanksgiving.* New York: Clarion.

Munsch, Robert. 1985. *Thomas' Snowsuit.* New York: Annick Press.

Murphy, Stuart J. 1996. *Too Many Kangaroo Things to Do.* New York: HarperTrophy.

Murphy, Stuart J. 1999. *Jump, Kangaroo, Jump!* New York: HarperTrophy.

Newman, Patricia. 2004. *Jingle the Brass.* New York: Farrar, Straus, and Giroux.

Nikola-Lisa, W. 2004. *Setting the Turkeys Free.* New York: Hyperion Books for Children.

Numeroff, Laura Joffe. 1992. *If You Give a Mouse a Cookie.* New York: HarperCollins.

Numeroff, Laura Joffe. 1998. *If You Give a Pig a Pancake.* New York: Laura Geringer.

Numeroff, Laura Joffe. 2004. *Beatrice Doesn't Want To.* Cambridge, MA: Candlewick.

Oldfield, Margaret Jean. 1969. *More Tell and Draw Stories.* Minneapolis, MN: Creative Storytime Press.

Olson, Mary W. 2000. *Nice Try, Tooth Fairy.* New York: Simon and Schuster Children's Publishing.

O'Malley, Kevin. 2001. *Humpty Dumpty Egg-Splodes.* New York: Walker.

Osborn, Susan. 1995. *A Pocket for Corduroy* (videocassette). New York: Good Times Video.

Palatini, Margie. 2004. *Moo Who?* New York: Katherine Tegen Books.

Parr, Todd. 2005. *Reading Makes You Feel Good.* New York: Little, Brown.

Payne, Emma. 1973. *Katy No Pocket.* Boston: Houghton Mifflin.

Peet, Bill. 1983. *No Such Things.* Boston: Houghton Mifflin.

Peet, Bill. 1979. *The Spooky Tale of Prewitt Peacock.* Boston: Houghton Mifflin.

Pfister, Marcus. 1992. *Rainbow Fish.* New York: North-South Books.

Pfister, Marcus. 2002. *Just the Way You Are.* New York: North-South Books.

Pilkey, Dav. 1990. *'Twas the Night Before Thanksgiving.* New York: Orchard.

Plourde, Lynn. 1997. *Pigs in Mud in the Middle of the Road.* Rockport, ME: Down East Books.

Polette, Keith. 2004. *Isabel and the Hungry Coyote.* Green Bay, WI: Raven Tree Press.

Prater, John. 2003. *Is It Christmas?* Hauppauge, NY: Barron's.

Quinn, Lin. 2001. *Best Mud Pie.* New York: Children's Press.

Rau, Dana Meachen. 2001. *Bob's Vacation.* New York: Children's Press.

Ray, Mary Lyn. 2001. *Mud.* San Diego, CA: Harcourt Children's Books.

Regniers, Beatrice Schenk de. 2003. *What Did You Put in Your Pocket?* New York: HarperCollins.

Reid, Margarette S. 1990. *The Button Box.* New York: Dutton.

Reider, Katja. 2002. *The Big Little Sneeze.* New York: North-South Books.

Relf, Adam. 2005. *Fox Makes Friends.* New York: Sterling.

Rey, Margaret. 1998. *Curious George Makes Pancakes.* Boston: Houghton Mifflin.

Rice, James. 1986. *Texas Night Before Christmas.* Gretna, LA: Pelican Publishing.

Rice, James. 1990. *Cowboy Night Before Christmas.* Gretna, LA: Pelican Publishing.

Riddell, Chris. 2002. *Platypus.* San Diego, CA: Harcourt Children's Books.

Ripper, Georgie. 2003. *Brian and Bob, the Tale of Two Guinea Pigs.* New York: Hyperion.

Riva, Renee. 2005. *Izzy the Lizzy.* New York: Waterbrook Press.

Robertson, Ivan. 2000. *Jack and the Leprechaun.* New York: Random House Books for Young Readers.

Romero-Stevens, Jan. 1999. *Twelve Lizards Leaping: A New Twelve Days of Christmas.* Flagstaff, AZ: Rising Moon.

Ross, Tom. 1994. *Eggbert, the Slightly Cracked Egg.* New York: G. P. Putnam's Sons.

Rothstein, Gloria. 2003. *Sheep Asleep.* New York: HarperCollins.

Rubel, Nicole. 2002. *No More Vegetables!* New York: Farrar, Straus and Giroux.

Sabuda, Robert. 1997. *Cookie Count.* New York: Little Simon.

Salley, Coleen. 2004. *Why Epossumondas Has No Hair on His Tail.* San Diego, CA: Harcourt Children's Books.

Sams, Carl R. 2000. *Stranger in the Woods.* Milford, MI: Carl R. Sams II Photography.

San Souci, Robert D. 2000. *Six Foolish Fishermen: A Cajun Story from Louisiana.* New York: Hyperion.

SanAngelo, Ryan. 2002. *Spaghetti Eddie.* Honesdale, PA: Boyds Mills Press.

Schafer, Susan. 2005. *Where's My Tail?* New York: Marshall Cavendish Children's Books.

Scherer, Jeffrey. 1999. *One Snowy Day.* New York: Econo-Clad Books.

Schwartz, Betty Ann. 2000. *What Makes a Rainbow?* Santa Monica, CA: Piggy Toes Press.

Scieszka, Jon. 1992. *The Stinky Cheese Man and Other Fairly Stupid Tales.* New York: Viking Juvenile.

Selby, Jennifer. 1997. *The Seed Bunny.* San Diego, CA: Harcourt.

Seuss, Dr. 1960. *Green Eggs and Ham.* New York: Random House Books for Young Readers.

Shannon, George. 1992. *Lizard's Song.* New York: HarperTrophy.

Shaw, Nancy. 1986. *Sheep in a Jeep.* Boston: Houghton Mifflin.

Shields, Carol Diggory. 2002. *Saturday Night at the Dinosaur Stomp.* Cambridge, MA: Candlewick.

Sierra, Judy. 1987. *Flannel Board Storytelling Book.* New York: H. W. Wilson.

Sierra, Judy. 1997. *Counting Crocodiles.* Orlando, FL: Gulliver Books.

Sierra, Judy. 2001. *Preschool to the Rescue.* San Diego, CA: Gulliver Books.

Sierra, Judy. 2004. *What Time Is It, Mr. Crocodile?* Orlando, FL: Gulliver Books.

Sierra, Judy. 2004. *Wild About Books.* New York: Alfred A. Knopf.

Silverman, Erica. 1992. *The Big Pumpkin.* New York: Simon and Schuster Children's Publishing.

Silverstein, Shel. 1981. *A Light in the Attic.* New York: HarperCollins.

Simmons, Jane. 2000. *Daisy and the Egg.* London: Orchard Books.

Simmons, Jane. 2001. *Daisy's Hide and Seek.* New York: Little, Brown.

Simon, Charnan. 1999. *Mud.* Brookfield, CT: Millbrook Press.

Singer, Marilyn. 2002. *Boo Hoo Boo-Boo.* New York: Harper Growing Tree.

Sloat, Teri. 2000. *Farmer Brown Shears His Sheep.* New York: DK Publishers.

Smyhem, Theresa. 2004. *Snowbear's Christmas Countdown.* New York: Holt.

Speed, Toby. 2000. *Brave Potatoes.* New York: G. P. Putnam's Sons.

Sperring, Mark. 2003. *Find-a-Saurus.* New York: Scholastic.

Spinelli, Eileen. 2004. *Thanksgiving at the Tappletons'.* New York: HarperTrophy.

Stangl, Jean. 1986. *Flannel Graphs: Flannel Board Fun for Little Ones Preschool–Grade 3.* Carthage: Fearon Teaching Aids.

Steig, William. 1997. *Toby, Where Are You?* New York: HarperCollins.

Stevens, Janet. 2003. *Jackalope.* San Diego, CA: Harcourt Children's Books.

Stickland, Paul. 1997. *Ten Terrible Dinosaurs.* New York: Dutton Juvenile.

Stickland, Paul. 2000. *Dinosaur Friends.* San Francisco, CA: Handprint Books.

Stockham, Jess. 2004. *Runaway Train.* Auburn, ME: Child's Play.

Storad, Conrad J. 2003. *Don't Ever Cross That Road, an Armadillo Story* Tempe, AZ: RGU Group.

Sturges, Philemon. 2001. *I Love Trains!* New York: HarperCollins.

Stutson, Caroline. 1999. *Cowpokes.* New York: Lothrop, Lee and Shepard Books.

Taback, Simms. 1999. *Joseph Had a Little Overcoat.* New York: Viking.

Tafuri, Nancy. 2000. *Will You Be My Friend?* New York: Scholastic.

Theobald, Joseph. 2003. *Marvin Wanted More!* London: Bloomsbury.

Thompson, Lauren. 2000. *Mouse's First Halloween.* New York: Simon and Schuster Children's.

Thompson, Richard. 1990. *Frog's Riddle and Other Draw-and-Tell Stories.* Toronto: Annick Press.

Totline. 2000. *The Best of Totline Flannelboards.* Waldoboro, ME: Totline Publications.

Trapani, Iza. 2001. *Baa, Baa, Black Sheep.* Watertown, MA: Whispering Coyote.

Vaughan, Marcia K. 2001. *We're Going on a Ghost Hunt.* San Diego, CA: Silver Whistle.

Vaughan, Marcia K. 2002. *Kissing Coyotes.* Flagstaff, AZ: Rising Moon.

Vrombaut, An. 2003. *Clarabella's Teeth.* New York: Clarion.

Waddell, Martin. 2005. *It's Quacking Time.* Cambridge, MA: Candlewick Press.

Walsh, Vivian. 2002. *Gluey, a Snail Tale.* San Diego, CA: Harcourt.

Ward, Helen. 2002. *Old Shell, New Shell: A Coral Reef Tale.* Brookfield, CT: Millbrook Press.

Warren, Jean. 1987. *Short-Short Stories.* Everett, WA: Warren Publishing House.

Warren, Jean. 1987. *Teeny-Tiny Folktales.* Everett, WA: Warren Publishing House.

Warrick, Karen Clemens. 2001. *If I Had a Tail.* Flagstaff, AZ: Rising Moon.

Watt, Melanie. 2001. *Leon the Chameleon.* New York: Kids Can Press.

Weeks, Sarah. 2000. *Mrs. McNosh and the Great Big Squash.* New York: HarperFestival.

Weeks, Sarah. 2003. *Two Eggs, Please.* New York: Atheneum Books for Young Readers.

Weeks, Sarah. 2004. *Baa-Choo!* New York: HarperCollins.

Wert, Faye Van. 2000. *Empty Pockets*. Bridge-port, CT: Greene Bark Press.

Weston, Tamson. 2003. *Hey, Pancakes!* San Diego, CA: Silver Whistle.

Whybrow, Ian. 1997. *Harry and the Snow King*. London: Levinson Books.

Wilcoxen, Chuck. 2004. *Niccolini's Song*. New York: Dutton Children's Books.

Wilder, Laura Ingalls. 1997. *Christmas in the Big Woods*. New York: HarperCollins.

Williams, Linda. 1988. *The Little Old Lady Who Was Not Afraid of Anything*. New York: HarperCollins.

Wilmes, Liz. 1997. *Felt Board Fingerplays: With Patterns and Activities*. Elgin, IL: Building Blocks.

Wilson, Karma. 2002. *Bear Snores On*. New York: McElderry Books.

Wilson, Karma. 2004. *Bear Stays Up for Christmas*. New York: McElderry Books.

Wing, Natasha. 2003. *The Night Before the Tooth Fairy*. New York: Grossett and Dunlap.

Winnick, Karen B. 2002. *Barn Sneeze*. Honesdale, PA: Boyds Mills Press.

Winters, Kay. 1999. *Whooo's Haunting the Teeny Tiny Ghost*. New York: Harper-Collins.

Wisnieski, Davis. 1997. *Golem*. New York: Clarion.

Wood, Don. 2002. *Merry Christmas, Big Hungry Bear!* New York: Blue Sky Press.

Yolen, Jane. 2001. *How Do Dinosaurs Say Goodnight?* New York: Blue Sky Press.

Yolen, Jane. 2005. *How Do Dinosaurs Eat Their Food?* New York: Blue Sky Press.

Ziefert, Harriet. 2000. *Train Song*. New York: T. Y. Orchard.

Zion, Gene. 1956. *Harry the Dirty Dog*. New York: HarperCollins.

Source C

PATTERNS FOR CRAFTS

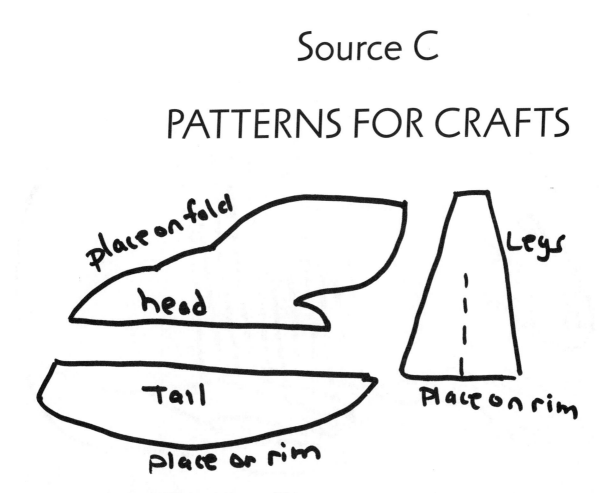

C-1: Paper Plate Armadillo Head, Face, and Feet

C-2: Armadillo Stick Puppet

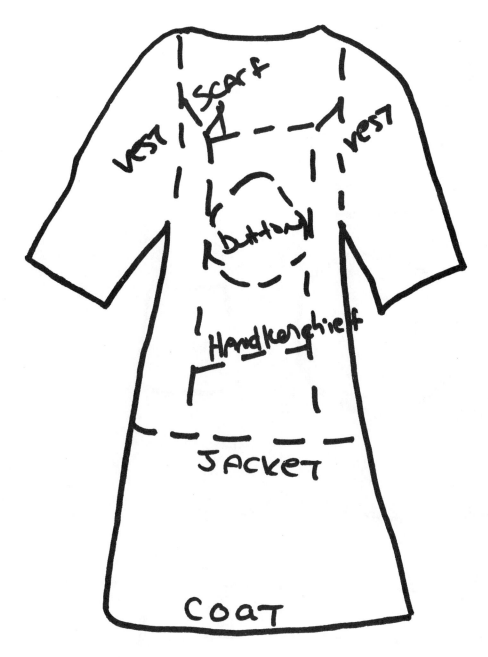

C-3: Button Up Coat

C-4: Crocodile and Monkey Figures for Door Hanger

C-5: Dinosaurs

C-6: Egg Man and Clothes

C-7: Guinea Pig

C-8: Bat and Ghost

C-9: Hermit Crab

C-10: Kangaroo

C-11: Lizard

C-12: Dog, Pig, and Duck Finger Puppets

C-13: Tooth Fairy's Coming

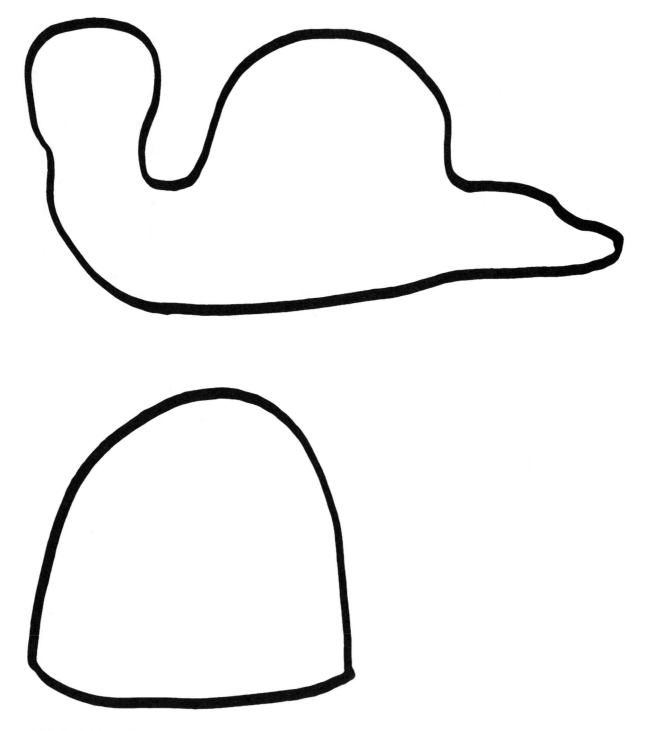

C-14: Snail Finger Puppet

C-15: Vegetables

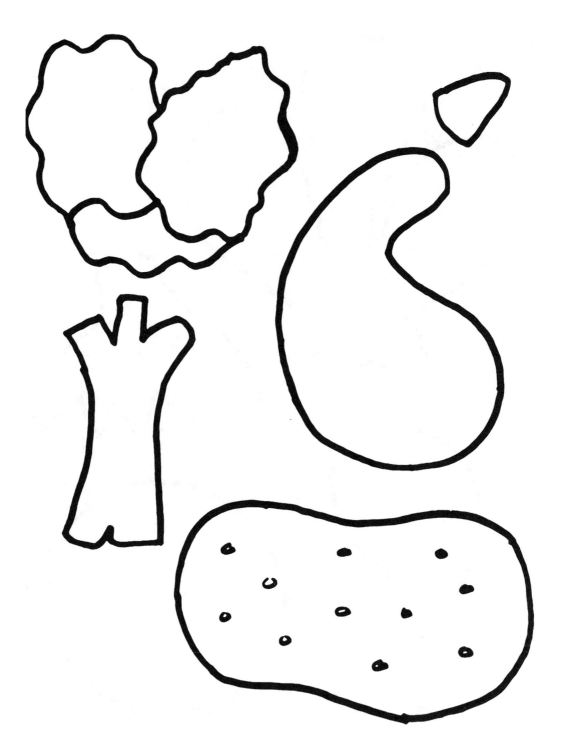

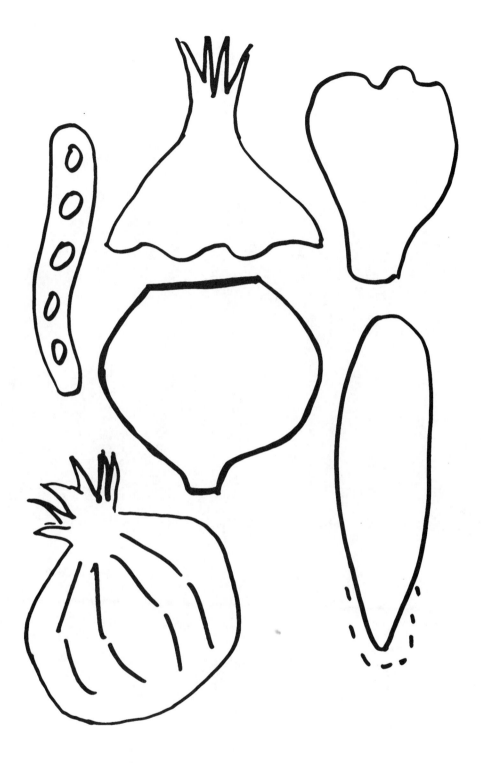

Source D

CRAFTS AND MATERIALS INDEX

INDEX

ABOUT THE AUTHOR

Kay Lincycomb worked as a consultant for several years planning storytime programs and summer reading programs work for the Rowlett Public Library, Rowlett, Texas. She then joined the system as a children's librarian, becoming a regular staff member in 2005.

Kay worked from 1983 to 1995 at Nicholson Memorial Library in Garland, Texas. She left for several years to work in the public school system as an elementary librarian, returning to Nicholson in 1999.

During her years as a librarian, Kay Lincycomb has worked with children from a few months up to middle school age; presented storytimes for babies, toddlers, preschool children, elementary school students, and school-age children. She has also performed puppet plays for special events.

Kay now lives in Rowlett, Texas, with her husband, Bill, two wonderful children, Traci and Cari, and three mischievous cats.